ASTROLOGICAL REMEDIATION:
A Guide for the Modern Practitioner

Published by Moira Press

Copyright © 2012 by the Moira Press
www.moirapress.org

Assisting and Editing by Sara Beth Brooks, Breana Cross, Susan Gehrz
Interviews with Judith Hill, Yoshihiro Matsuoka
Cover Design by Groshong Erickson
Cover Photo by Scott Gerke

All rights reserved. No part of this publication may be reproduced without the author's permission, except the inclusion of brief quotations.

ISBN 978-0-9827893-2-2

I could not have created this book without
these very talented individuals.

Interviews
Judith Hill
Yoshihiro Matsuoka

Editing
Sara Beth Brooks
Breana Cross
Susan Gehrz

Book Cover
Groshong Erickson
Scott Gerke

*May we continually rise up to the
silver-lined tips of our essential soul,
finding open receivers for each
of our bountiful gifts.*

For my precious Angelene

Table of Contents

1. An Introduction to Astrology — 1
2. Remediation: a Primer — 9
3. On Radical Astral Freedom — 20
4. On the Ethics of Examining, Predicting, Diagnosing, Suggesting, and Prescribing — 29
5. A Beginning into the Art of Astrological Remediation: Goals, Tenants, & Methodology — 41
6. Astral Prevention: Remediating before suffering takes hold of the Mind, Body, or Spirit — 52
7. Remediation, as it acts upon the Physical, Mental & Emotional Spheres — 59
8. On the Link between Astrology & Medicine — 67
9. Astrological Diagnosis — 75
10. Isolating the Planets that need Remediation — 83

Remedial Schematica   90

11. The Planets in Remediation   91

     11.1 The Sun 92
     11.2 The Moon 95
     11.3 Mercury 104
     11.4 Venus 114
     11.5 Mars 118
     11.6 Jupiter 122
     11.7 Saturn 125
     11.8 Uranus 130
     11.9 Neptune 133
     11.10 Pluto 140

12. The Signs in Remediation   142

13. The Houses in Remediation   147

14. The Aspects in Remediation   152

Remedial Technique   172

15. Symbolic Substitution   173

16. Strategic Planning as Remediation   200

17. Astral Loving: Vibrational Merging as Remediation   208

18. The Art of Astrally-timed Information, Love, Assignments, Advice, and Assistance   217

Advanced Considerations   **224**

19. Is Astrology Inherently Fate-Based?
    An Interview with Judith Hill   225

20. Babies & Children: Considerations   251

21. The Supreme Art of creating
    Win-Win Situations   265

22. The Subtle Art of Glorifying
    Stressful Configurations   267

23. On the Gory Nature of Certain Remediations   281

24. On the Remediation of Addiction   285

25. Food Love: An Interview
    with Yoshihiro Matsuoka   296

Navigating Transitions   **304**

Extras..316
Glossary...317
Works Cited..320
Afterwords..326

Foreword

The appearance of a sophisticated text on western astrological remedials is cause for celebration. For decades, the psychological and spiritual uses of astrology have reigned, deepening and broadening our science. Now the time has come to remind the student of the practical utility of astrology. The utilitarian branches of astrology dominated the field from ancient times, up through the mid twentieth century. However, this book does more than reiterate ancient techniques. Ms. Gehrz has achieved a unique paradigm on remediation, promulgating a new school of astrological thought. She has detailed a mindset and process *behind* inventive remediation.

When I first met Andrea, I was amazed. She is the only person I've ever met who reads ancient Greek, is a highly sought after American Sign Language interpreter, and who had taken the time and money to go to Kepler College in pursuit of an astrology degree. Who else had this precise mix of rather odd credentials?

Over tea and a myriad of fun cooking experiments, Andrea would muse ineffectually about translating some Greek works one day, as she was equally distracted by her musical pursuits, motherhood, and a score of other interests. Make no mistake, Andrea is a true polymath.

Following my vehement kitchen lecture series on the topic of "the obvious reason you were reborn," Andrea shaped up and completed her outstanding translations of *An Introduction to the Tetrabiblos of Ptolemy*, by Porphyry of Tyre and *Anthology: Book One,* by Vettius Valens of Antioch, in less than one year.

The comfortable clarity of these recent translations has awakened both the delight and curiosity of the astrological world and these first books are just the beginning. It is my humble opinion that we have witnessed the appearance of a welcome light in the history of our craft. Cutting her teeth on the translations of ancient Greek astrological texts, this volume before you represents the first fruits of Ms. Gehrz's original thought.

Rather than providing a "cookbook" approach to remediation, Gehrz leads the reader through a tour of concepts, mechanics, and possibilities of astrological correction. She shows the would-be practitioner how to think! After all, the greatest remedialist is an intuitive mechanic. Without this skill, we astrologers are mere describers, impotent to help someone alter or shift a negatively presenting natal or transit problem. Our prevailing enamourment with the psychological implications of astrology has overshadowed the study's historic status as a radically effective helpmeet in all manner of human conditions. Today, most folks are ignorant of astrology's remarkable capacity in vocational selection, medicine, location, agriculture, fertility, and scores of other important life endeavors.

Astrological Remediation: A Guide for the Modern Practitioner, brings into the spotlight a new approach for an imminently realistic and healing use of the astrological birth chart. May we feel gratitude towards our collective heritage, and the astonishing mind that has birthed this remarkable and vastly influential work.

Judith Hill

Preface

This tome has been welling up inside of me for many years.

When I read my first astrology book, it felt as if I had finally discovered language for the vibrations I had been experiencing my entire life. With the discovery of astrological timing techniques, such as the use of transits and progressions, I began to track these energetic shifts, and was able to correlate them to the planetary movements. I could then keep track of how they affected my body, mind, and thoughts. Since coming into the study of astrology, I have deeply pondered the mechanism behind its magical and profound workings. Any student of the subject has surely been amazed by the exactitude and precision of astrology, in the timing of future and past events, internal struggles, bodily illness, and the subtle, passing moods that sweep through us in any given day.

It is the unending and uncanny accuracy of astrology that keeps me motivated to continue my study. On account of its exactness, I also believe that astrology can be used to aid in healing. For instance, the use of medical astrology can often be as accurate as a laboratory test, yet looking at the astrological chart is completely noninvasive. The analysis of an astrological chart can also be used as a technique for precise diagnosis.

After working as a professional astrologer for ten years, there came a point at which I could no longer stand idly by, observing the malaise and joy brought with the ebb and flow of planetary energies. I have watched these waves move through my own life, as well as the lives of my friends, and clients. I had often felt like a helpless observer. I craved some sort of method to heal and help during periods of great planetary duress, and to optimally channel positive energies into their highest possible manifestation. The moment I birthed my gorgeous daughter, this need to transmute and heal upcoming energies became even more urgent.

I still vividly remember the moment I sat perusing my ephemeris, only to notice that Saturn would be coming up to square my daughter's natal sun, along with transiting Uranus, Mars, and the Moon. As an astrologer and new mother, this was quite upsetting, as her body was still tiny and so very new to the planetary energies. This onslaught of astral forces was sure to be unpleasant for her. It was at this point that I began my life as an astrological remedialist.

Since my daughter's birth, I have devoted a great amount of time learning how to use astrology as a tool to remediate suffering of all kinds. This subtle paradigm shift has been imperative for my happiness as a mother, partner, friend, and practicing astrologer. It is my goal in the book that follows to share everything about astrological remediation that I have learned through my own experience, practice, and observation. Within this book lies the fruits of my labor.

Andrea L. Gehrz

1

An Introduction to
Astrology:

(also known as....)[1]

---

[1] The study of planetary vibrations, astral mechanics, and the schematic language of celestial energies.

As I attempt to set out a beginning into the art of astrological remediation, I feel it necessary to clarify some basic operational definitions. Although it is my assumption that most readers of this book will already be familiar with the complex language of the astral forces, I welcome readers who are new to astrology as well. It is my hope that both budding astrologers and seasoned professionals can find something of use within these pages.

Let us begin with the question:

What is Astrology?

> *Astrology is the study of how the movements and placements of celestial bodies affect emotional, mental, and physical life on earth.*

There are many branches of astrological study. Psychological, evolutionary, relationship, and horary astrology are all common. The possibilities are truly endless. One unifying characteristic found in all branches of astrology is the use of planetary positions to analyze aspects of earthly existence. The astrological chart itself can be likened to a symbolic diagram with the ability to convey a great deal of information. The exactitude and nature of the information gleaned from the chart will depend upon a number of factors. The mental and emotional framework of the astrologer reading the chart is one of the most important considerations. The information conveyed will depend on what is currently happening within the systems indicated by that chart, and how this information is filtered through the lens of each astrologer.

This process could be likened to two different auto mechanics reading the same electrical diagram for a car. The available information regarding the layout of the electrical circuitry for the car would be exactly the same in both cases. The manner in which each mechanic uses this information will be a bit different and depend upon the symptoms present in that car, as well as the specific training and experience of each mechanic.

Astrology could also be understood as the language of the vibrations being emitted from the planets. For the purpose of this book, we will need to understand how these planetary emissions affect *people* physically, emotionally, mentally, etc. The exact mechanism of astrology is still unknown, yet there is quite a bit that is known about how to write down and examine the energies that are streaming in from the celestial sphere. This is where the astrological chart comes into play.

An astrological chart is a symbolic portrait of the celestial realm at a specific time, which provides us with a picture of the vibrations being emitted from the cosmos at that precise moment. The astrological chart functions as a schematic diagram of the celestial bodies, and shows us the areas of life through which planetary energies present themselves. As astrologers, we examine how changes in planetary movements affect emotions, behaviors, and the overall trends of people, animals, plants, countries, etc.

Now let us examine the importance of the astrological chart for the moment of an individual's exact date, time, and place of birth. In modern times, the chart for the exact time of birth is most often called the *natal chart*. The chart for a person's birth will indicate the positioning of the celestial bodies at the specific moment in which that person was born into the terrestrial world. This chart can be used to examine the specific and ever-evolving needs of an individual soul, at any given time in the life; such as but not limited to, the practical, emotional, sexual, and medical needs. The natal chart can be thought of as a map of a person's vibration, the state and tendencies of that person's astral and physical body, and the areas of life into which the soul will be pulled. The natal chart is also the schematic diagram through which a passionate and dedicated astrologer can understand the celestial realm, in order to attend to the needs of an individual soul.

We could propose that each person has a vibrational pattern which is locked within their DNA, cells, soul, and heart. This vibrational pattern is indicated by the astrological chart for the moment of birth. One function of astrology about which we know very little, is exactly *how* these astral influences combine within and affect us.

* * *

At this point, I think it best to introduce a new term. In the previous example, analyzing a chart was likened to an auto mechanic using an electrical schematic to study the wiring within a car's engine. A computer network administrator might also look at the schematic diagram of a computing network in order to see how different servers and machines are communicating with one another, within the system of that network. We find schematic diagrams all around us everyday, as we look at metro transit maps, repair manuals, assembly instructions, and astrological charts.

Let us now suppose that the astrological chart could be called the *astral schematic*.

The planets within the astral schematic represent the energies within the system of the cosmos. For instance, the placement of Mars could be said to show where heat might be coming into the body, while Saturn will show the location which tends to become overly cold or constricted. Mars could be likened to the spark plugs within an engine, while Saturn could be thought to represent the cooling system. The zodiacal signs in the astral schematic filter energy within the astral body, indicating the manner in which the planetary energies will flow in and out of certain parts of the auric field and physical body.

The houses in the astrological chart show the areas of life into which the energies of the astral body are focused, as they are filtered through the twelve signs. Aspects (angles between the planets in the astral schematic), show the connections between the energy emitters within the system, indicating which vibrations can and will mix together.

Astral Schematic[2]

The *astral schematic* is a diagram of the celestial bodies for a specific moment in time, and can be examined as a depiction of the vibrational essence and evolution of a person, animal, or any other enlivened being.

The astral schematic is composed of planets, signs, houses and aspects.

* * *

Planets = energy emitters

Signs = the filters through which the planetary energies are emitted

Houses = the domains of human life from and into which the energies of the planets are emitted

Aspects = the geometric configurations of planetary energies

---

[2] Schema, Schemata

$τὸ\ σχῆμα,\ ατος$ = Form. Shape. Figure

1. Particular Configuration
2. Character. Characteristic Property
3. A Figure or Drawing
4. Geometrical Figure

*A Greek-English Lexicon by Liddell and Scott p1895

For the purpose of this book, let us now familiarize ourselves with the term *hypostatic schematic*. Ancient Greek astrologers often used this term to describe the chart at birth. The term *hypostatic* literally means, "unchanging and underneath." The natal chart could be said to be unchanging, inasmuch as parts of our nature stick with us throughout the duration of our lifetime.

The **Hypostatic Schematic** can be described as follows:

The ***hypostatic schematic*** is the astrological chart, which lies unchanging and underneath.

The hypostatic schematic is a pictorial diagram of the celestial moment at which a soul has finalized congealment into the physical form.

The hypostatic schematic is the static chart that lies underneath the moving energies of the traveling planets.

Personalities, tendencies, and patterns continuously evolve over time. The natal chart seems to indicate the filter through which we receive and perceive the human experience. The natal chart is essentially a pictoral representation of this emotional geometry. The evolution of the self can often be seen through the astrological *progressions*. Progressions allow us to track and observe the evolution of the essence, nature, and life experience of each individual soul. As planets orbit through space forming geometric configurations with the planetary positions in the natal chat, their emissions affect us by mixing with our natural, internal vibration. This is the phenomenon of *transits*. A transit can be thought of as a vibrational transition, caused by the moving planets.

The Hypostatic Schematic[3]

The *hypostatic schematic* or "natal chart," is a diagram of the planetary positions at the moment of birth. When discussing the natal chart, the ancient Greek astrologers often used the word "hypostasis," which is a conceptually loaded and fascinating word.

Now let us deconstruct the word itself.

Hupostasis/ὑποστασις = *Hypostasis*

Hupo = Hypo = Under   Ex: *Hypodermic needle*
                        A Needle that goes under the skin.

Stasis = Standing Still. The quality of being stationary

   Ex: Static vs. Dynamic = Unchanging vs. Changing

---

[3] Hypostasis

ἡ ὑπόστασις = a standing under. a supporting.
   1. in liquids: that which settles to the bottom; sediment.
      2. an accumulation of pus.
         3. a jelly or thick soup.
      4. the quality of coming into existence; origination.
         5. a foundation or substructure.
      6. the groundwork; the subject matter.
         7. an undertaking.
      8. substantial nature; substance.
         9. existence; reality.
            10. real nature.

*A Greek-English Lexicon by Liddell and Scott p1895

2

Remediation: A Primer

****

[4] *Secret Envelopes.*

Within each *Secret Envelope* is a remediation for a challenging time in the future. They are intended to be opened either directly before, during, or just after certain transits. While the goal of each envelope is entirely unique, the common thread is that each envelope uses the art of future prediction, by use of astrology, in order to *help in advance*.

Astrological remediation is the use of any method necessary to heal and soothe existing problems, as indicated within the chart. This includes problems that have existed from birth, or have come in through the moving vibrations of the traveling planets.

This book will focus its discussion on the use of astrology and the analysis of the astral schematic in order to heal problematic energies. A unique characteristic of astrological remediation is that it inherently examines and accepts the vibrational foundation of the individual who is seeking help. Astrology could be described as a detailed study of individuality. Astrological remediation could be understood as an endlessly fascinating journey into highly individualized healing methods.

The primary purpose of medicine and medical care is to remedy what ails us. There are various methods of health care, all of which are meant to heal or help. It is a great blessing that astrological remediation and modern medicine can exist simultaneously. There is no cognitive dissonance here. Within the framework of astrological remediation, a person who is ill or suffering can be healed by any number of methods.

The concept that we are souls residing within a physical body is common within the astrological community. We can obviously see, talk to, and touch other people in their human bodies. It is less obvious that each and every enlivened being is also made up of an astral body, which could be thought of as a person's aura, chakra field, emotional-energy-body, etc. Some people have the ability to see the enrgey-bodies and auras of others. A person may also discern this same information through a process of feeling another person's astral body in some manner, such as through psychic methods or an extreme sensitivity to the energetic subtleties within another person's field.

A person who cannot inherently perceive the astral body can discern information about another person's energetic state by observing their behavior, especially when the emotional expression is pronounced or intense. For instance, if we see a child who is crying and screaming, this most likely indicates that the child is upset or sad. But it could also mean that the child is scared, frustrated, or sick. If we want to discern the reason why the child is upset, we may need to use our natural instincts and intuition, to appeal to and affect change within the child's energy-body. It is within this energetic body that illness begins, and in order to truly heal the physical body from certain illnesses, the energetic problem underneath must also be dissipated.

In her timeless book *Hands of Light*, Barbara Ann Brennan describes clearly the energy-body and the existence of illness as a reality that begins within the vibrational field. The energy-body is very much connected with the soul. Astrology provides us with a language that we can use to explain and describe the needs and tendencies of the energy-body.

The symptomology might also show up through certain actions that seem to work against the higher needs and wants of an individual. For example, suppose there is a man in his mid-forties who seems entirely unable to commit to a long-term relationship, even though marriage and children have been the single most important dream throughout his entire adult life. Maybe he has always wanted a wife and children, but every time he finds himself in a healthy, happy relationship he instantaneously becomes commitment-phobic and flees. One way to treat this problem would be to deal purely with the behavior of "fleeing."

Several different approaches could be used in an attempt to heal this detrimental behavior. Behavioral therapy, one-on-one counseling, or discussing the problem with friends could all prove to be effective solutions. The man himself might try to remedy the problem through a repeated pattern of self-deprecating or shaming thoughts, during which he beats himself up over and over about his constant and unending ability to "control himself." While all of these methods do in fact try to attack the problem, none of them have yet looked into the underlying energetic difficulty that is leading to the odd behaviors in the first place.

With astrological remediation, we will want to know *why* these behaviors keep occurring. And the *why* here may be very deep and at times surprising. The astrological chart of the fleeing man might show that the problem is caused by an unusually sensitive energy body. This could mean that every time he intimately bonds with a lady, he begins to feel everything that she is thinking and feeling. He then starts to experience suffocating sensations, or a feeling of not knowing what is real and what is not. These feelings lead the man to the idea that something about the relationship is crazy-making. As a result, the man flees in order to escape the feelings of suffocation and resurrect the ability to perceive and differentiate his own emotions and thoughts.

The remediation for this problem would have to be energetic, because the man's auric field happens to be very sensitive to the vibrations of others. A gem or stone that alters the energy-field to be less porous, or less apt to absorb outside energies, may be of great help. Maybe the astrological practitioner could prescribe showers or swimming as methods of cleaning and clearing the man's energy-field, so that he might be able to better handle and manage outside energetic influences. A flower essence or homeopathic remedy might also be helpful.

Now suppose that the same exact symptoms were to show up in the case of a woman who wanted to commit to a relationship but could not. The behaviors might show up in an almost identical manner to the overly sensitive man.

As soon as the woman settles into a healthy relationship, she ends up fleeing almost immediately. A look at the woman's astrological chart might indicate that the problem stems from a very different energetic combination. Let us suppose that the woman were to have an extremely hot and excited Mars, sitting together with the very electric planet of Uranus. Every time the woman were to experience a vibrational influxing to this part of her chart, she would unexpectedly feel excited and inflamed. These hot and electric feelings would lead her to get cranky with her boyfriends, unexpectedly cheat on them, or even break off these relationships entirely. In this case, the remedy would be very different than in the situation of the overly sensitive man.

As mentioned, the astrological remedial for the sensitive man might be something to block other people's vibrations from getting into his field, such as a stone or amulet. In the case of the wily and excitable woman, the remedy would need to treat her overheated Mars, perhaps by cooling it off while also providing a healthier outlet for her overly rebellious side. An astrologer might prescribe an athletic outlet to this woman, such as boxing or mountain biking. The goal here would be to find an activity that would satisfy the riled-up cravings of her soul, but in a manner that would be less destructive to the emotional relationships in her life.

Astrological remediation is an extremely useful method of healing, because it inherently approaches each situation as unique, and attempts to understand and fix the energetic root of the problem at hand, using a variety of methods. By healing the energetic difficulty that lies underneath the problematic behaviors, the symptomatic behaviors themselves can truly be allowed to change, or begin to fade away.

Astrological remediation was common throughout the ancient traditions, yet seems to have become a sparse topic of discussion and writing in the modern, western thought structure. In the eastern traditions, remediation has been consistently used and developed throughout the centuries. A traditional Indian astrologer might prescribe the use of certain gems to remedy problems within the chart, or prescribe a mantra to her client in order to mitigate the harsh qualities of a certain period of time. A spiritual pilgrimage to a sacred site may also be prescribed for a problem deep within the soul. In medieval times, astrological remediation was often practiced through the use of talismans, amulets, alchemy, and spells.

Having provided astrological readings and remedial suggestions to a large number of clients, I was at first tempted to write lists of successful astrological remediations for each and every possible planetary configuration. Because the nature of astrological remediation is to honor each chart as entirely unique, it has instead become my goal to teach the reader *how* to think about remediation, so that each student and practitioner may compile a list of his or her own remedies. Healing of both the physical and emotional body can happen through a chiropractor, dentist, or nurse. A suitable remedy could also be found through a volunteer job at the local senior citizen's center. A list of remedials can be as sparse or as extensive as necessary for each particular scenario and should always be inventive.

In many cultures, shamans have the ability to heal the energy-body by communing with other realms in order to relay messages from the spirit world. These messages are then passed along to help heal the injured parts of a certain person's soul. Astrological remediation could be seen as a cousin of shamanism. Within the scope of astrological remediation, the chart can be used to analyze and discover the exact nature of the symptoms presenting, and the soul can then be healed through this study.

Astrological remediation could most simply be described as, "the use of astrology in order to heal people, make life more enjoyable, and release suffering." The process of astrological remediation can be quite technical and precise, yet healing seems to also be inherent in the nature of simple astrology itself.

In newspapers, overly-simplified, sun-sign columns show up each and every week. While true astral scientists do at times scoff at the distillation of astrology into the twelve character types of Aries, Taurus, etc., this basic analysis of human character does lend itself to the acceptance of differences, and the twelve signs do seem to account for many of the temperamental differences that cause people both grief and joy. I can't count the number of times I have heard clients say things like:

I am never dating a Gemini again! They are so boring and predictable.

My girlfriend is so clingy! It is probably because she has four planets in Sagittarius.

My dad was a Taurus and because of this I grew up learning how to go with the flow, accepting change with open arms.

These comments make me chuckle, as oftentimes the traits being described are in exact opposition to the actual traits associated with the astrological sign being spoken of. The healing effect here is profound nonetheless. Notice that the client here is not blaming their ex-girlfriend for being boring, but instead, they are blaming the fact that the ex-girlfriend is a Gemini. This way of thinking replaces a criticism of the person's internal character, with an acceptance that the manner of being is innate on account of the sign involved. In this example, we see only one of the truly profound healing gifts that the astral sciences provide.

The emotion of shame exists within all human beings. Most cultures use subtle tools of shame and blame in order to guide people into accepting shared realities. Shared realities can be thought of as anything that a certain culture or group accepts as normal. People who have held internal desires that work against this reality have been shamed in many ways. Shame could be defined as a feeling or belief that one is inherently flawed in some way. A common experience among people who cannot fit into or conform to societal norms is a feeling of frustration and inferiority.

Modern psychology often contributes to the shame cycle. This occurs mainly on account of the dichotomous thinking between normal and abnormal psychology. Assessment and labeling of people with psychological disorders is one manner of adhering to shared realities. Within the modern psychological system of thinking, anomalous behaviors are classified into a pendulum of "normal" vs. "not normal." Astrology is one of the few sciences in existence that does not require a comparison to normalcy. The celestial vault judges no one. It knows no gender, race, diagnosis, or label. The celestial realm is within us. It pulses within our internal universe. In doing so, the energies of the stars create an entirely unique experience within each and every enlivened being.

Because astrology is a unique and complex study of individuality, it can provide a non-judgmental analysis of behaviors that might seem altogether impossible to understand. Certain vibrational patterns can be quite bizarre. It takes a very special kind of person to walk up on a high beam during a huge construction project. Someone makes our toothbrushes. Another person flies airplanes. It takes a certain temperament to do many jobs. Dentists don't seem to mind pulling teeth out of people's heads.

It could be said that:

Nothing in life is ever a detriment unless it is expected to be something else.

This brings us back to the remedial gifts that are borne from a study such as astrology. We have all had the experience of going to a clinic or emergency room, only to have a medical professional ask us fifty contrived and scripted questions, vaguely listen to our answers, and then prescribe us medicine. To some individuals, this is a form of remediation. From an astral point of view, understanding the patient's medical and qualitative make-up, before prescribing a method of healing, is an important step missing from this equation. Without this information, it is very hard to truly remedy a problem.

Many forms of modern medicine can be used to cover up or mask symptoms, but rarely do they release the energetic blockage that has caused or contributed to the problem at hand. The healing methods employed by a remedialist can and will take on a variety of forms.

Remediation could be a placebo pill. It could be a massage. It could be a hearty round of parcheesi while listening to the neighbors fight over their toy poodle. In certain very stressful situations, the least offensive remediation might even take on the form of a makeover, complete with plastic surgeries and a new face. Whatever the case may be, it could be proposed that a combination of modern and allopathic medical services and astrological insight can successfully aid in healing the body, mind, and spirit.

Astrological Remediation

Astrological remediation is the use of the
schematic language of celestial energies to
heal and soothe the spirit.

Astrological remediation is the act of healing the
energy-body through the use of the astral schematic.

Astrological remediation is the use of
the symbolic language of floating vibrations
in order to alter hard vibrations
into more harmonious ones.

Astrological remediation can take on the form
of anything in the earthly realm that will soothe and heal
the specific needs of an individual soul, whether the
method be allopathic, astrological, artistic, cerebral, etc.

Astrological remediation is the study of understanding
and altering a person's vibrational make up
in order to heal or soothe that person.

Astrological remediation is the study of
astral mechanics in order to repair problems in the
auric field.

Astrological remediation is
Heart Medicine.

3 On Radical Astral Freedom

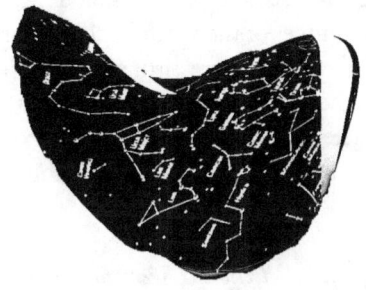

The subject of "fate vs. free will," has been a passionate and frequent topic of debate within my immediate astrological community.

Free will can most simply be defined as:

> *The freedom to exert one's will.*

In relation to astrology, free will could be thought of as the freedom to be in charge of one's own planetary energies, existence, destiny, future, karma, and life experiences.

A common assumption is that astrology functions based on the idea that all things are preordained in the astrological chart from the moment of birth. It is clear that the "fate vs. free will" spectrum is one which must be carefully considered by each astrologer.

This reminds me of a conversation I once had while attending Kepler College for Astrological Arts and Sciences; a place where I met a number of thoughtful and scholarly astrologers. One night, a few of us were sitting around in the student lounge. Throughout the night, we collectively came up with the idea that fate and free will can in fact exist at the same time. A fellow student used an example to convince me of this fact, stating:

Suppose in a political election, I were to vote for the candidate that I truly wanted to win, but the election had been rigged. The ultimate outcome would have already been decided, yet I would have also made my choice. In this case, the choice would have also already been fated for me.

Among ancient Greek astrologers, there was often a fate-based philosophy underpinning the astrology that was practiced. This type of thinking tends to scare modern students of astrology, who seem to hold tightly to the idea that we are entirely in control of our life experience. There exists the larger cultural belief that people have limitless options when it comes to using their free will, and can essentially pick and choose whatever it is that they might want to do throughout life.

In reality, the truth is most likely a mix of both fate and freedom. Our futures are probably a combination of certain fated occurrences that can coexist with a certain amount of freedom to choose. There seem to be certain relationships and events within any life that feel as though they are meant to be. With this understanding in mind, we can more easily accept that there will be energies and karma acting upon and within us as we move into our futures.

With this in mind, it should not be assumed that using astrology's techniques in order to predict certain future occurrences is a defiant act. Or even that we as astrologers shouldn't enjoy the eerie accuracy of astrology's ability to predict events of all kinds.

As a practicing astrologer, it has been necessary to develop language about these concepts. My clients often need some language about free will, especially after witnessing the accuracy of astrology's past predictions. Astrology's uncanny precision can leave a client feeling shocked at the seeming fatedness of everything. Each astrologer must of course discover his or her own beliefs in this area. It is my particular belief and experience that when used correctly, astrology can be one of the most healing studies in existence, but in order to truly heal, we must use a *radical free will* approach as we engage in astrological analysis. Let us call this philosophy *radical astral freedom*.

Radical Astral Freedom

The act of living as if we have the utmost level of
personal freedom and choice, in order to act gracefully
within, throughout, and alongside the planetary energies.

The *radical astral freedom* approach can be likened to certain martial arts that work with the energies of one's opponent. These martial arts do not make the assumption that the opponent is not filled with energy. The teachers of these disciplines instead instruct the martial artist in the skill of harnessing his opponent's chi, and using this energy for the fighter's own protection. This could come in the form of an opponent running at a fighter, who then uses the forward motion of his opponent to flip him onto his back.

Within the radical astral freedom approach to astrology, the planetary energies are to be worked with, harnessed, used, floated upon, and even enjoyed. At times, and always for the greatest good of all involved, the planetary energies are also to be deflected, manipulated, and altered.

One very healing aspect of astrology is its ability to bring clarity to traumatic, past events and allow for the clearing out of harmful energies. An astrologer's past predictions can act to clean out residual painful and difficult experiences. Astrology is the perfect language for understanding and identifying thought structures that are not allowing energies to flow in and out of the energy-body. The reason for this lies in astrology's tendency towards non-judgement, coupled with its extreme accuracy in predicting things that have happened in the past.

Watching the future through a fated lens can be an ultimately futile act. The subconscious anticipation of seeing so many transits coming up to trigger events in the charts of my clients, has at times felt like a great burden. I have found it ultimately healing and uplifting to adopt the aforementioned radical astral freedom approach to astrology.

This philosophy also removes the burden of the astrologer to "prove" astrology to the skeptical client. Instead, the chart can be approached as if it is a schematic diagram of the client's tendencies and vibrations, and the method through which the astrologer can read the chart begins with an inquiry into the client's past. Questions about the past can be used in order to discern how the client has used his or her qualities up until this point. Through this process, astrology will naturally reveal itself as a precise and intricate study.

Dissecting past experiences with a client allows many positive things to happen. The astrologer has become familiar with the chart by studying its earthly manifestations, while the client becomes familiar with astrology and its uses. Through this past-oriented process, the fatedness of these experiences could be said to be true, inasmuch as the client had yet to learn the vibrational under-workings of their very own chart. If the client had no knowledge or control of their planetary energies up until this point, this combination of factors could make past events seem as though they were indeed "fated."

Once the astrologer has delved into enough past patterns to understand how the client has been expressing the particular energies of his or her chart, the upcoming influxes of transiting energies can be examined through the lens of radical free will. In other words, the astrologer and the client can work together in order to find useful and effective remedial measures for any challenging energies that might be awaiting the client in the upcoming weeks, months, and years.

As we can see, a radical astral freedom approach will allow the client to make choices about how he or she will want to use both challenging and pleasant vibrations in the future. One method of dealing with such upcoming influences would be to "fate it out," meaning that one could chose to wait out a hard time gracefully until the energies pass[5]. Another option would be to vigilantly remediate the upcoming challenges with stones, mantras, or some other sort of remediation that would change or alter the vibrations entering the life. Another option would be to channel the energies outward and through the body, so they do not fester in the energetic field. The astrologer could assist the client in maximizing the feelings accompanied by such influences. One way to do this would be to manipulate one's surroundings to inherently support and encourage the energies to flow in a positive way.

As these examples demonstrate, astrology has the ability to provide a positive outlook, inasmuch as the future is an exciting opportunity for change, stimuli, and vibrational renewal. Regardless of the exact mechanism for astrology, whether spiritual, purely scientific, or mechanical, when taking the radical astral freedom approach to astrology, all things are malleable.

---

[5] This is similar to the ancient Greek philosophy of Stoicism, in which astrology was seen as being useful inasmuch as it could help in preparing a person for their upcoming "fates." In this way, a person was seen as being able to most gracefully handle the circumstances of life, as they could be watching them simultaneously, "*as above so below.*"

If we assume that astrology is in fact successful at predicting certain feelings, events, or energies in the life, and we also accept that these energies are to be managed, handled, and even dissipated through certain remedial measures, then we will have arrived at a very effective and helpful way to use astrology.

> **Fate it out:** *To gracefully wait out painful moments of a seemingly fated period of pain and suffering.*

Example: *Fate Style*

A client comes into our office.

We see that she has recently experienced transiting Pluto, Neptune, Uranus, and Saturn aspecting her natal Venus. Suppose we begin the session by asking the client if she has just experienced an intensely idealistic, yet erratic and distant time period in her relationship. Suppose we even look through the ephemeris in order to provide the exact dates on which the strife began. The client may look at us wide-eyed and say:

Yes, how did you know!?

One option would be to respond:

Because it was in your chart.

This answer inherently communicates to the client the idea that the chart is a map proving that most things in life are fated. Even though we as astrologers might not explicitly say it, the client will usually assume this. The ability of astrology to time events can be so precise that the chart appears to be entirely fated.

In *fate style* astrology, the next step is often then to predict what will be coming up in the future. When leaving things up to the "hands of fate," the astrologer is at the mercy of what is written in the chart. If the planetary configurations look stressful, the astrologer can often feel helpless. Yet if we tweak our thinking a bit, we easily find productive uses for difficult energies without attempting to divert or deflect them.

Example: *Radical Astral Freedom Style*

Suppose the same client comes into our office.

We see that she has recently experienced transiting Pluto, Neptune, Uranus, and Saturn aspecting her natal Venus. Again, we ask her if she might recently have had an unexpected, confusing, intense, and separating time period in relation to love.

Within the framework of radical astral freedom, we will of course reassure the client that her relationship troubles could not have been avoided entirely, as she was under the influence of extreme and love-related planetary duress. This will instantly release some of the internal feelings of shame that she may have been dealing with since the trauma of her recent experience. We can mention that we are excited to work with the client in order to create a brighter future. At this point, we can offer to use any means necessary to help this happen.

Each client is different. Healing could happen in the form of self-understanding, boundary-building, community-building, creating a brighter narrative, suggesting activities, helping the client open up to happy relationships, etc. What the client needs will depend on their chart. Saturn might need release. Uranus might need a conductor for it's electrical surges. Because each client is having their own unique experience, we will talk to each one of them differently. The overall goal of the radical astral freedom approach is to create a brighter future through the process of creatively working with the energetic qualities of the planets.

4

On the Ethics of Examining, Predicting, Diagnosing, Suggesting, & Prescribing

Throughout the course of this book, we will in fact learn how to heal problems in the natal chart. Before we delve into the finer techniques of remediation however, we must first learn the art of not creating sorrow ourselves through the act of performing astrological readings. During my many years of studying and practicing astrology, I have yet to meet an astrologer whose heart was not genuine, but this topic must be considered nonetheless. Whether or not we understand it, as practitioners of the divine art of astrology, we hold a sacred responsibility to uphold good thoughts in the minds of our clients. When we have a client's life map in front of us, we are being entrusted with the power to help them understand who they are, who they have been thus far, and who they can be in the future.

And thus, the first lesson in the art of astral mechanics is to:

Do No Harm

This is easier said than done. Yet there are many ways that we can begin to think about the subject. First of all, it must be recognized that there exists a power differential between the astrologer and the client. This power dynamic shows up in many professional relationships, those in which one person holds a greater amount of information or technical skill than the other; such as between a doctor and patient, or a lawyer and their client.

In any situation in which there exists a power differential, the person with less knowledge is giving themselves over to the consulting individual. In the case of a lawyer/client relationship, the client cannot navigate the court system without the aid of an attorney. Neither can our clients read their astrological chart without the aid and expertise of the astrologer.

In the same way that a doctor or lawyer follows a code of ethics, so shall we as remedialists. Any serious remedialist would be wise to get acquainted with the code of ethics laid out by the Organization of Professional Astrologers. The OPA addresses the issues brought up here by suggesting that:

Every astrologer take full responsibility for the information he or she is imparting, and that every client be treated in a thoughtful, sensitive manner. This includes refraining from making statements that may be stressful to the client and that may not be true, such as predicting someone will never marry, never have children, or die at a specific time[6].

We do not want to suggest that our clients are destined for horrible futures. In fact, the only good reason to look into the future is to help create a brighter one.

Borrowing from ethical codes in other disciplines, we can learn even more about ways in which to avoid incidentally hurting our clients. We can do this by attempting to always:

> *Describe our role as remedialists clearly to clients.*
> *Accept jobs only of which we are qualified.*
> *Ask for appropriate and clear compensation.*
> *Maintain client privacy.*

These are just a few thoughts on the ethics of remediation. As the field of astral healing continues to grow, a formal code of ethics will surely be written. Until that time comes, we as remedialists can continue to uphold a high ethical standard within our own work.

There does not exist a school for astrological remediation, yet we can still be creative in the ways which we continue to learn. Developing and practicing our own methods will advance the field organically. Each remedialist is probably best served by applying his or her already existing areas of expertise to the art of healing through use of the astral schematic.

---

[6] For a reference to this statement and much more, visit the site for the OPA at http://www.opaastrology.com/about/code-of-ethics.

For instance, if a remedialist is also a musician, then music could be used as a method of healing. One simple method of musical remediation would be to send a CD of beautiful songs to someone who is under extreme planetary stress. Another method might be to give a young child an assignment to practice rudiments on a transit from Saturn to Venus.

Another remedialist might have a sustained interest in medieval latin scholarship, and might best grow as a remedialist through a study of astral alchemy. These methods could then be used in their applications towards astrological healing. No two remedialists will ever examine an issue through the exact same lens. This is a cause for celebration! The healing potential of astrology is infinite. A personal style is best chosen by a study of the gifts and strengths lying within the chart of each and every remedialist.

This book assumes a pre-existing knowledge of astrology and will not focus on the technicalities of reading a chart. It will instead support and teach ways to use astrology as a positive force for humanity. In fact, a whole book could be written on the subject of *doing no harm*. Each astrologer must find his or her own style of gracefully interfacing astrological foreknowledge with the need for people to be in control of their own destinies. While we cannot possibly attempt to address every ethical consideration in one chapter, we have at least made a beginning into a discussion of the subject. One way in which astrologers may incidentally cause malaise, is through the (most often accidental) act of *non-supportive futuring*.

Non-Supportive Futuring

Informing the client of difficult upcoming or existing astrological configurations in a manner that does not allow for a productive understanding of how to optimally navigate them.

A few ways we can hope to avoid non-supportive futuring are to not:
> *Suggest that horrible things might happen.*
> *Look aghast at something in the chart.*
> *Assign negative labels to parts of the chart.*
> *Give the client no choices about their future.*
> *Describe hard energies without framing*
> *the information in a useful manner.*

Because of the power differential between the client and the astrologer, it will be very important to focus our efforts on a philosophy which we will call *supportive futuring*. The premise behind the supportive futuring approach is that astrology shall always and in every case be consulted for its most useful purposes.

Supportive Futuring

The act of using astrology and its timing techniques in order to educate, support, and aid the client in finding optimal uses for all of their energies.

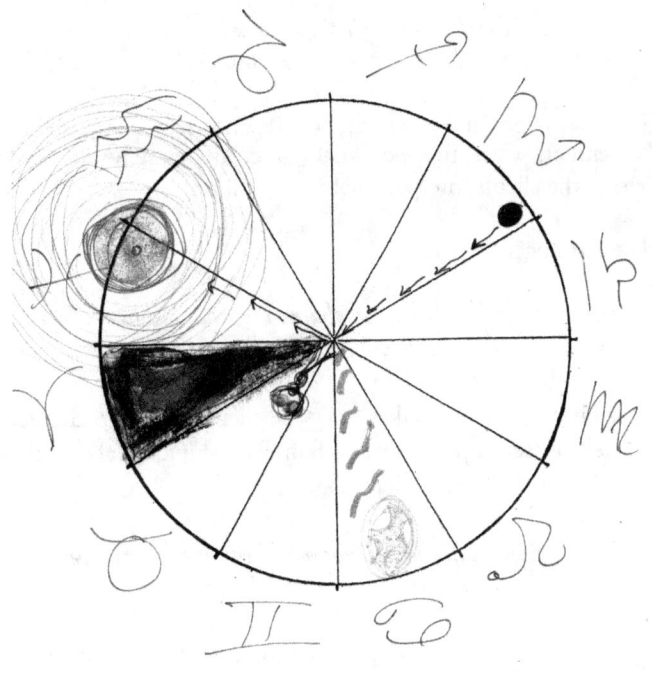

Sun in Pisces, Moon in Cancer, Aries Rising at birth.

Mars: Scorpio

Now let us illustrate these concepts through an example. Suppose a client were to come into an astrologer's office and ask the following question:

> *Will I end up marrying the person I have been dating for the last six months?*

The astrologer looks at the chart and sees a transit in November, with the potential to create extreme turmoil within the clients interpersonal relationships.

The astrologer then says:

> *No. There is a good chance the relationship will end in November.*

This kind of response takes away the client's power to choose, as well as sets up a morbid frame of thinking about the situation at hand. The client asks:

> *Should I remain in the relationship until the transit is over, or should I break up with him?*

In order to provide for supportive futuring, the astrologer may then positively respond with:

> *I am happy to describe the potentials of the relationship over the long term. By knowing what you might expect over time you can then be prepared to make a more informed decision.*

This of course is only one example. In any field, ethical considerations are often the most challenging, as they require the use of both critical thinking and problem-solving skills. There is usually no one right answer, and at times some options could be deemed as equally positive or negative.

Methods to ensure Supportive Futuring:

1. Re-phrasing questions that force the astrologer to make a decision for the client.

> **Ex:** Client: *Should I move to Chicago or Brooklyn?*
>
> Astrologer: *Would you like me to check the astro-cartography results and describe the vibrational atmosphere you will experience in each location? This might be quite practical in helping you make an informed decision.*

2. Focus on giving good options and language for any energy in the chart (as opposed to the use of conventional labels).

Ex of labeling language:

> *Mercury square Uranus is so unfocused!*

Ex of positive language:

> *Mercury square Uranus is electric.*
> *A mind such as this is perfect for creating new ideas!*

3. Assume that bright futures are possible under any kind of astrological weather, and that it is the astrologer's goal to guide the client into the best possible use of each unique time period.

When a client asks a question that poses an ethical dilemma, we must ask ourselves why they are asking the question in order to uncover the intent behind the inquiry. Refusing to answer certain questions, without guiding the client to a better understanding of why they are asking the question in the first place, could leave them feeling rejected or ashamed. One technique that might be quite useful in this case would be to rephrase the question into an alternate inquiry; one that is ultimately beneficial for the client. We want to help guide them to a better understanding of themselves and the answers they seek, with kindness, wisdom, and grace.

We will also want to observe the mental and emotional filters through which the questions are being asked. If a different person were to ask the same exact question, the context and knowledge base of that person might be entirely different. For instance, if the inquiry were to come from a student of astrology who had thoroughly studied the composite chart and synastry of a partnership, he might be asking for a second opinion. In this case, the most supportive future might be created from a true analytical examination of both charts. It is important to understand the intent and context behind each question in order to provide supportive and productive answers.

For any person having relationship stress (or any other kind of stress for that matter), it could be very healing to point out upcoming transits which will bring with them the potential for great excitement and joy. This might mean finding a nice Jupiter transit to talk about, or perhaps the next trine from Uranus, which will bring a freeing vibration in some area of life. There is always something good coming in the future!

Let us take the example of the client from the previous page. Suppose we see that transiting Saturn has been squaring her natal Venus. This will tell us that she may have been enduring a period of great stress in her romantic relationship. In this case, the intent of the question might be to get confirmation that everything will be okay and that the relationship will endure. She is also most likely wondering whether or not the current hardship in the relationship will persist. If we sense that this is the intent, then perhaps we could address the question like this:

It does look like you have been under some relationship stress for the past few months. Let me look into the future to find some more joyful time periods. During these periods of opportunity and abundance, you will be supported vibrationally in mending your current relationship. If you do choose to end things with your current boyfriend, these time periods will aid in healing and integrating the changes you have made.

Because astrology is the study of individuality, the exact manner in which to create a supportive future will be different with every client.

There are many considerations involved in the ethics of reading charts. While the topic of ethics could grow into an entire text, there are many basic ethical considerations to remember. If a client were to show up in our office asking us to look into the chart of the person they were dating, it would be unethical to do so without the other party's permission. This is one manner of upholding an ethic of good boundaries and privacy. We do not want to deeply analyze the psyche of another person without asking. This act could be likened to looking into someone's car window, or even into their underwear drawer.

Often astrologers will ask for written permission in the case that someone wants another person's chart to be analyzed. When dealing with ethical consideration, there are always exceptions to the rule. There might be situations in which it is in fact contextually appropriate to look into a person's chart without their consent. Many astrologers will consult parents about the charts of their children up until the age of 18 years old. When done gracefully, this can be a very healing use of astrology.

With adults, there might in fact be certain situations in which viewing a chart without consent is an act of utilitarianism. In other words, at times this action can support the happiest future for all involved. Suppose there was a single mother with two children who was considering dating a man she had met on the internet. It can easily be understood that the vibrational quality of the mother's relationship will affect the lives of her children. A quick analysis of how this single mother will get along with with someone born on the same day as her potential date will provide a great deal of information about the future possibilities of such a union. This use of astrology could function as a preventative screening method for internet dating. In this situation, we are viewing a theoretical chart. We are not using the potential date's birth time. In this way, we are not looking into his soul, but instead into the energies of the day he was born.

When we are examining charts without direct consent, there must be a very good and ethical reason behind this act. It must be done with the utmost care to maintain integrity throughout the process. In the example above, it will also be very important to stick to a description of a theoretical composite chart, and not to go into a detailed description of the internet date's birth chart with the client. This would be a direct intrusion into his privacy, while a look at the composite chart is a look into one possible future.

Because no ethical consideration is ever cut and dry, it is important to use careful consideration when dealing with tough questions, such as those presented here. At times clients will be experiencing problems for which there is no immediate or perfect answer. It is in the best interest of any astrologer to cultivate and have confidence in their personal philosophies in order to deal with such situations.

Utilitarianism has been discussed as a neutral yet ultimately loving thought structure, as it does not hold within it a judgmental framework. Instead, a situation that is weighed under the scales of utilitarian thinking will always be analyzed with the greatest good in mind. Each astrologer will be helped by a higher philosophy that can bring light in the case of extremely hard choices.

As remedialists we must aim to always heal and never harm. When handling ethical considerations, our intent must be pure.

5
A Beginning into the Art of Astrological Remediation:

Goals, Tenants,
&
Methodology

---

[7] An *Envelope Project Show* on December 17, 2010. Artists from Portland, Oregon created art to research and celebrate the sun, mercury, venus, and mars traveling through the sign of Scorpio! See page 201 for a detailed description of this event.

Now that we have established a solid foundation in the philosophy of radical astral freedom, and an understanding to do no harm, we will now begin with a description of the most basic goals of astrological remediation. We will also introduce Judith Hill's *Tenants of Astral Mechanics,* and introduce a few possible methodologies for remediating charts.

Let us begin this process by introducing the five most important goals for the astral mechanic, as created and explained by Judith Hill in the tenants appearing in the pages that follow. It could be said that an astral mechanic attempts to maximize the potential utility and happiness of any astrological chart. This transformation can occur on many levels and through methods which are infinite in scope. The manner in which we will heal ourselves and our clients can be revealed through an uncovering of the astral tendencies involved, and an inventive foray into maximizing the essential nature. Within the pages of this book, we will attend to the following five goals.

Goals of Astrological Remediation

Strengthen the character and will.

Open the heart to its highest wisdom.

Optimize the physical constitution.

Enhance the mental process and narrative.

Maximize the potential and scope of the good deeds.

Judith Hill on Astral Mechanics

I prefer to call the field of astrology something more along the lines of *astral-mechanology*. Or even better, we might call it astral mechanics because that is exactly what it is! Astrology is a holistic yet mechanical process, engaging all levels of a human being. Although this approach is not entirely lost within modern astrology, it certainly could benefit from a loud revitalization. By understanding the planets as emitting temperature, tone, and color, each of which have a function, the interpreter is freed from absolutist interpretations. Personally, I prefer to practice a healing-focused study of astral-mechanology, meaning that as an astral mechanic, my focus is on researching the celestial mechanism inasmuch as I can help and heal through this process. Let us go ahead and write out some simple definitions.

Astral Mechanology: The study of the celestial mechanism and its effects as they are reflected within earthborn organisms (especially but not limited to humans) and the earth herself.

Astral Mechanics: The act of manipulating these astral vibrations in order to repair and fix vibrations that might negatively affect such humans or the earth herself.

Tenets of Astral Mechanics·
by Judith Hill

1. The study and practice of astral mechanics understands the solar system as emitting light forces, vibrations, and chemical effects of various kinds. These influxes then act in wonderful and mysterious ways upon this dense earth plane and its creatures.

Within the framework of astral mechanics, the planetary birth chart (or *astral schematic)* displays the life field, forces, potentialities, and tendencies of a particular life.

The astral schematic does not however show the eternal spirit inhabiting this life experience. Nor does it show the choices that the inhabiting spirit will make, nor how it will choose to use its planetary equipment.

The cosmically-originating vibrations indicated in the astral schematic also combine with an individual's life situation, culture, historical time period, character, proclivities, level of spiritual advancement, and personal karma.

The essential guiding factor of evolution remains the eternal spirit, with its helpmeets of the mind, the heart and the will.

2. The philosophy behind astral mechanics accepts the soul as the inhabitant of the body, as well as the doctrine of reincarnation. These concepts are neither required nor necessary, in order to engage the scientific mechanism of astral mechanics.

3. The philosophy behind astral mechanics accepts that we are born at the exact time that best represents us. As in, we have participated in creating our initial birth chart, inasmuch as our chart is now participating in creating our current experience.

4. The study and practice of astral mechanics assumes that the influence of the planets function by the transfer of vibration through color, temperature, tone, water molecules, metals, and light rays (as opposed to good and bad and pre-decided theoretical influences).

5. The study and practice of astral mechanics accepts the existence within humans of an *astral receiver*. The solar system is also understood to be linked immediately and intimately to this receiver.

As in, an astral mechanic accepts the idea that the cycle of one's inner Venus follows the cycle of the big Venus in the heavens. They are as one.

6. The study and practice of astral mechanics recognizes the existence of both positive and negative cosmic influences and accepts that suffering exists as a real experience upon the earth plane.

7. The existence of the field of astral mechanics inherently assumes that a human being is designed to understand and alter planetary energies.

The manipulation of energies is understood to be constructive or destructive to the individual or society involved, depending upon the manner in which energy is used or altered.

8. Astral mechanics does not wholeheartedly assign the judgement of "good" to benefic planets and "bad" to malefic planets.

While recognizing good and bad energies as earthly realities, these positive and negative influences are determined individually in each case by observing the unique circumstances of planetary strength, house, and sign position. Then, by noting the admixtures of rays with other planets. The same planet may be strong for one activity and ruin another, or assist a house while itself being weak; or be "positive" but acting in excess, etc.

9. Astral mechanics see the art of prediction not necessarily as "prediction" but instead as a viable "a +b = c" outcome.

Future occurrences are dependent upon the sort of seeds that are planted in each individual's garden. These seeds are understood to hatch under specific planetary weather systems. Outcomes then may be multifaceted and variable.

10. Astral mechanics recognizes fate, karma, and destiny as real, but variable according to each situation and each individual case.

11. The practice of astral mechanics recognizes that the human will must be seen as the "boss" of the urges and proclivities that inherently stem from the planetary influxes.

The focus then is not on the fated parts of the life, but instead on enhancing and strengthening the will, the nature of the thoughts, the ability to love, and the deeds within any given life.

12. The study and use of astral mechanics supports the understanding of and conscious use of planetary energies for the healing and evolution of mankind.

13. Practitioners of astral mechanics recognize that only a tiny amount is known about planetary research at this point. We are open to both scientific and intuitive research in this field.

14. The fundamental principles of astral mechanics can exist simultaneously with all other interpretive branches of astrology; natal, medical, vocational, esoteric, psychological, comparative, locational, agricultural, etc.

15. The study and practice of astral mechanics builds upon both ancient and traditional uses and understandings of astrology.

16. The practice and use of astral mechanics does not require that the practitioner view the planets in a religious context, use them as "Gods," nor even "messengers of God."

17. The work of an astral mechanic is to study and practice the art of manipulating planetary energies in order to transmute karma and relieve suffering. The following processes may be used to alter problematic vibrations;

> Neutralization
> Transfer
> Substitution
> Deflection
> Balancing
> Attraction
> Enhancement
> Absorption

18. Astral Mechanics are free to accept that God's grace precludes both astrolic influences and remedials and can operate above and beyond either.

Now that we understand the basic tenants behind the art of astrological remediation, let us now take a look into a few possible methods for handling challenging planetary configurations. In certain sections throughout the book, these methods will be employed, yet as we know, the various ways in which we can heal and soothe are endless!

Methodology

Symbolic Substitution

Symbolic substitution allows energetic neutralization, deflection, transfer, absorption, etc., to happen through worldly activities that naturally satisfy the soul-needs. Certain un-channeled needs might cause unwanted behaviors or physical symptoms. In symbolic substitution, we will use a very simple, two-step process. The first part of the process will be to locate the energetic cluster in the astral schematic which is causing the unwanted patterns. The second part of the process is to find activities and outlets into which the problem-causing vibrations can most gloriously be channeled. By finding an apt place to pour one's abundant energies or honor one's constricted vibes, we create a veritable landscape upon which to become a more centered, productive, and happy version of ourselves.

Vibrational Enhancement through Energy-Mixing

By allowing other vibrations to mix with our own we can neutralize, absorb, or even enhance certain parts of ourselves. This process could be likened to that of communing with another person, animal, town, etc. By bringing new energies into and around ourselves, we inherently alter our own life sphere. This is one of the most fun ways to remediate hard parts in our own charts! By spending time with people we love, who validate and heal the hardest parts of ourselves, we can ensure brighter futures through vigilant love remediations of all kinds. We can also alter our lives by moving to a new town; one which has different qualities from the one in which we have been feeling stagnant. New vibes can even enter our fields through short trips. It could be suggested that this is how the use of stones or metals work as well. Each element or mineral vibrates at a different frequency. Keeping these objects on our person will surely change the tone, color, and quality of our vibrational fluxings.

Uplifting the Mental Framework

Because our mental states affect how we interface with the rest of the world, it is quite important to maintain a healthy, happy narrative about one's life. As astrologers, we can uplift humanity through the inherently non-judgmental lens of the astral sciences. We can do this by speaking to the highest potential in the charts of our clients and giving supporting, productive language to difficult energies. As astrologers, we have the blessed opportunity to provide a positive framework about even the most challenging of struggles!

Enhancing the Future

This is the simple art of checking theoretical charts in order to prevent long-term negative situations. Astral discernment can be employed through the use of composite charts of future dates, friends, caretakers of our children, future business partnerships, etc. This can also mean checking astro-cartography information before moving to a new town, or setting personal deadlines that are optimally-timed to our own charts. We can also engage the art of timing gestures of love to arrive at exact moments when we know that a person might need a bit of care because of a difficult transit. This could be as simple as sending an "I Love You" text when we know a friend's chart is under extreme duress.

Intention-Building through Talismans, Amulets, etc.

It could be said that concepts live in the same world as the unseen realm. This is the world of concept-formation. Free will might be thought of in this context as the ability to make one's own thought forms. A talisman or an amulet is often made from metal, but it can also be made from a substance as simple as paper. The most important part of making an amulet is often the clarifying of one's intentions that occurs through the process. As in, once we clarify our intention (i.e. the thought-picture of what we want to manifest into reality), we can then make that happen in the physical realm. Also, talismans are at times imbued with the vibrations of certain planets, as they are made under the emissions of these bodies themselves. In this way, they alter the energy field of the soul.

Strengthening the Physical Constitution through the use of Medical Astrology

Because an astrological chart is representative of our "photonic make-up," it also shows the parts of our physical structure that might tend to get compromised. A look at the astrological chart can give us clues into what might be contributing to seemingly undiagnosable illnesses, diseases that are erratic in nature (often attributed to Uranus), etc. We can also use the astrological chart as a lens through which to find possible remedies for what is ailing the physical structure. For instance, if the problem is coming from Neptune, we will use a bit more finesse, employing methods such as aromatherapy and tenderness. If the ailment is a broken bone, we would go with a structural enhancement such as a cast.

6 Astral Prevention:

Remediating
before suffering takes
hold of the
Mind, Body, or Spirit

We will now look into the art of examining qualitative time in order to avert suffering before it takes hold of the mind, body, or spirit.

Astral Prevention

The art of anticipating upcoming astral events in order to ameliorate problems in advance.

Prior preparation can minimize suffering during transits and allow individuals to feel empowered to handle upcoming challenges. Remedial prevention can be likened to taking an ibuprofen as soon as a headache starts in order to "nip it in the bud." It is much harder to soothe pain that has already taken hold of the body, mind, or heart. By attending to the struggle early on, we can attempt to walk through any experience with grace and style.

One way to avert highly stressful energies and prevent suffering from taking hold is to arrange for activities that will be suitable for the upcoming vibrations. In this way, the energies of the transits will be allowed to flow through the field, instead of incidentally causing unwanted problems. Another method of remedial prevention would be to stock up on herbs and tinctures that could be helpful under upcoming astral weather.

Suppose a client will have an upcoming Saturn transit, during which the body might tend towards a weakened ability to assimilate minerals into the bloodstream. We remedialists will want to make sure that the person is stocked up with herbal teas, such as oat-straw and nettles, or prescribe other methods to aid in mineral absorption. While Saturn can indicate periods of constriction and depletion, Mars can bring the problem of overheating. For example, if it appears that a child will be getting extremely hot in the next month, we might want to send him or her to school in an outfit that consists of layers. This way, the child can self-regulate the body heat. In excessively hot charts, such as in the case that a child has many planets in the fire signs, overheating can lead to behavior problems, sniffles, rashes, crankiness, and various other symptoms.

The driving concept at the core of remedial prevention is that astrology can help us anticipate certain life experiences and allow an opportunity to dance with the energies, maintaining a state of balance and grace. The options for working with upcoming energies are endless. A self-employed person may be able to plan the activities of each day according to what is coming in the chart, thus allowing a maximum potential for success. A parent can plan activities according to a child's chart, inasmuch as the chart will show the areas in which the child is seeking to expand and grow.

One simple use of astrology to prevent suffering in advance is to plan family trips or other important events according to the astral weather. Electional astrologers do this for many of life's important events, such as weddings and real estate purchases. Next is a list of some events and daily activities which can be maximized through the use of astrological timing techniques.

1. Good times for working hard and taking care of business.

2. Good times for relaxing and taking a day off.

3. Good times to meet people and be charming.

4. A good day for a wedding.

5. The ending of all kinds of sadness and malaise.

6. Weak times for the immune system.

   (During which we can boost our immune system by eating well and taking care of ourselves.)

7. Good times to receive or perform energy work.

8. Good times to promote oneself or start a publicity campaign.

9. A good time to have a job interview.

10. Good time periods for dating.

11. Times during which work might be frustrating, or we might need to pace ourselves.

12. Good times to go shopping.

Let us now take a real life situation for which a knowledge of the upcoming astral weathers will be useful. Suppose there is a family that is wanting to go on vacation. Now suppose also that one of the children in this family can at times be emotionally volatile, tending to fly off the handle for no apparent reason. If we look into the child's natal chart and see a natal Mercury-square-Mars configuration, we know that vibrational influxings to this part of the chart may very well indicate strife. A very practical form of astral prevention would be to time vacations and important events to *not* occur at times when this aspect would be inflamed.

Timing and planning for difficult transits allows for prevention of the most creative kinds. The limit of preventative possibilities depends only upon the innovation, openness, and experience of each and every astral mechanic.

If the chart indicates a future upsurge in creativity, we might want to prioritize making time to channel art during that period. Under the influence of Saturn, we may want to prepare to mold something tangible, as this could lessen the internal stress. Writing secret love notes to oneself to be opened on a later Saturn transit would be another option to deal with the constriction.

Directing stressful vibrations into concrete action, is one way to apply the technique of symbolic substitution. Through symbolic substitution, we seek to alter the manner in which a person will be expressing tense vibrations. If the body can be allowed to move and morph along with the energy field, then the experience of suffering might truly be averted. While it is most likely impossible to avert suffering entirely, the use of astrology can in most cases lessen the magnitude of suffering.

Buddhist philosophy suggests that the first step towards peace is to accept that suffering exists. It could very well be the case that suffering is inherently a part of the human experience, and the ability to rid a person of all suffering is an impossible task.

Astrology does inherently accept the idea that there is suffering, especially on account of the planet of Saturn. The cooling and condensing vibrations of Saturn often cause elevated levels of emotional and physical suffering. Astrologers must accept the fact that every chart contains a Saturn. The ancient Greek astrologer Vettius Valens explains the planet of Saturn as follows:

*Saturn rules **ananke & agnoia**[8].*

Ananke and Agnoia:

The natural condition of being constrained or limited by what we do not yet know by direct experience.

When thinking about the role of Saturn, it would seem a negation of the human experience entirely if one were to not

---

[8] ἀνάγκη = force, constraint, necessity.
necessity in the philosophical sense.
a natural and necessary condition.
compulsion exerted by a superior, for example.

ἄγνοια = want of perception, ignorance.
to not know something or not understand it.
to have yet to experience something directly.

Greek-English Lexicon, Liddell & Scott, 12 & 101

struggle at all. It could also be proposed that there are a number of methods through which to gain the knowledge and experience required by Saturn. If we are to believe that we have the utmost level of astral freedom, then it is assumed that we do have a choice of how we want to use the focused vibrations of Saturn. If Saturn must constrain us, then we can choose how we want to be constrained.

One symbolic substitution might be to physically constrict the body part which Saturn is affecting. It is important to note that the act of symbolic substitution does not inherently remove all of the discomfort that exists under Saturn, but it does lessen the magnitude of suffering, frustration, and shame, and allow us an opportunity to not take our ignorance personally.

7

Remediation, as it acts upon the:

Physical, Mental, and Emotional Spheres

Throughout many years of performing astrological consultations, I have noticed a very profound trend. The moving influences of the transits and progressions can and will manifest on a number of levels (emotionally, behaviorally, mentally, and physically). While not every sphere of life will be affected during every transit, the changing vibrations do tend to be thorough in their effects. The planets act upon our essence, and in this way they influence our entire being. Because the natal chart does affect our experience so deeply, the astral arts are a perfect medium through which to begin any healing process. We can work towards a holistic framework of balance and happiness by attending to all needs in life, as they are indicated in the natal chart. It is critical to closely examine hard aspects in the chart. These energies often present challenges on many levels. The example that follows is an illustration of the holistic approach that *is* astrological remediation. By examining an astrological chart, we can attend to the past, present, and future of an individual on a number of levels.

Example:

Natal Sun at 15 Leo
    square
Natal Mars at 15 Taurus

Transiting Neptune arrives at 10 Aquarius, beginning its long-lasting opposition to the Sun and square to Mars.

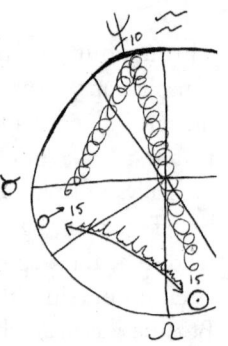

Neptune softens up both the Sun and Mars!

We know a few things immediately:

1. **Past condition -** *Natal Sun square Mars*: This person has historically been erratic and high energy in reference to his identity, general nature, physical constitution, and personality.

2. **Current condition -** *transiting Neptune*: He is beginning to feel more lethargic on account of Neptune's influence. The energy that is being brought to the natal planets by the transit

is very different from the energies in the natal chart. In fact, Neptune's needs seem almost antithetical to the needs of Mars. This vibrational mixing will most likely affect the physical, emotional, and mental health.

3. **Future condition - *transiting Neptune passes*:** There will be a point when the transit ends by passing off of the aspect. This will be in a few years. At this time, the life will go back to being more like it was before, but this man will also never be quite the same.

We as remedialists can begin to address the various facets of these hard energies by acknowledging the past, and talking about the nature of the chart *before* the current transit hit. By engaging in past prediction we can reassure the client that our future thinking will also be valuable.

This man will have been inherently changed by the transit. His life story will now include a new chapter. We as remedialists can aid in the healing process by explaining the energies at work and attempting to remove self-judgement and fear. In order to deal with some of the emotional and mental manifestations of the transit, we can provide information about what is happening in the astral schematic, as well as its manifestations in the life. Perhaps we could say something like:

The Sun in Leo is square to Mars in your natal chart. This brings a natural heat to the physical constitution, at times causing flare ups of one kind or another. It is as if the physical body and identity-self become inflamed, and you receive an erratically-timed burst of energy. This energy has been witnessed to come out in verbal fights and an inability to sit still. Also, there can be flare ups of sexual energy with this aspect, inasmuch there is an over-flare up, and perhaps the sexual energy is given in a way so that it spills out and overflows at times. Let's go back in time a bit to examine a few time periods in which this natal aspect was getting some planetary activity, as this should show us how the energy naturally has functioned in your life.

We then look in our ephemeris for any memorable or powerful transits to the natal aspect in the recent past. If the timing of a notable Saturn transit is too far back to remember, then we can look at the last time Mars or Jupiter hit the aspect. When we find dates that match up, we can then ask the client how he has noticed the tendencies to manifest.

We can then listen to the client as he describes his experience of the natal aspect. After we time a recent and memorable Mars transit to the Sun/Mars square, the client says:

*Oh yeah at times I can get pretty riled up.
During the time you mentioned, I got in a fight at the bar.*

Having this information, we can then move to the current transit at hand. We might say something like this:

As we can see, this square between your Sun and your Mars presents some needs that can be erratic at times. When an expansive energy comes in and hits your natal Sun and Mars, it will be easy to feel exceedingly optimistic in reference to the abilities of your physical body. One of the most difficult things for people to understand about squares is that the nature of a square is to be erratic and irregular. Currently, a new energy is coming in to alter this natal vibration, so let's articulate the nature of this sleepy, snuggly, lethargic, allergic-feeling, vibration, that Neptune brings.

This vibration is now beginning to mix with your normally vital yet unruly Sun square Mars. Neptune hitting the Sun will soften and dissolve the hard lines of the self-identity, while Neptune hitting Mars can bring all kinds of weird and strange feelings, including paranoia and itching.

In an emotional context, the feelings can also be that of disgust or the feeling that comes when a person has stayed up way too late, is really tired, yet has to much internal energy to fall asleep. These feelings, as well as the feeling of not quite understanding the identity as strongly, nor the needs of the physical body, have begun in the past few months. Have you been experiencing anything that feels like this?

Suppose then, that the client were to say something like this:

Lately I have been feeling very fatigued, and actually started itching. I am dating a new woman, but the whole thing is very confusing, as I am not even sure if I want to have sex with her, especially now that I am having this itching problem. She has a cat and I am allergic, so that is also causing a bit of a struggle. When I am at her house I get allergic and then I feel sleepy and lethargic.

As astrologers, we have now been able to understand some of the past behaviors of the natal aspect, as well as the manner in which the aspect is functioning currently under Neptune. We can then begin to envision appropriate remedies for the client's physical, emotional, and mental health. Here are a few possible examples for this particular client.

Neptune/Sun/Mars Remediations for Physical Health and Well-Being

1. Going swimming.

2. Taking up an energetic martial art such as qi gong, tai chi, aikido, etc.

3. Taking allergy medicine for the cat problem.

4. Attacking the itchy problem with home fermented foods, or some other remedy according to the entirety of the chart.

5. Acupuncture (can release heat build up).

6. Doing hot yoga or stretching in the shower.

Remediations for Emotional Health and Well-Being

1. Taking a homeopathic remedy for the emotional repercussions of the itching problem.

2. Enjoying new emotional and sexual concepts.

3. Understanding the higher needs and purpose of the transit by asking a wise elder, an expert, the highest self, or God.

4. Introducing certain forms of sexual illusion into the life, such as role playing or acting.

Remediations for Mental Health and Well-Being

1. Knowing that the weird feelings will not last forever.

2. Knowing the month and year that the energies will pass.

3. Knowing that the celestial vault is not judging us.

4. Deconstructing ideas that are inciting shame and guilt.

5. Releasing ideas that are contributing to cognitive dissonance.

8

On the Link Between
Astrology & Medicine

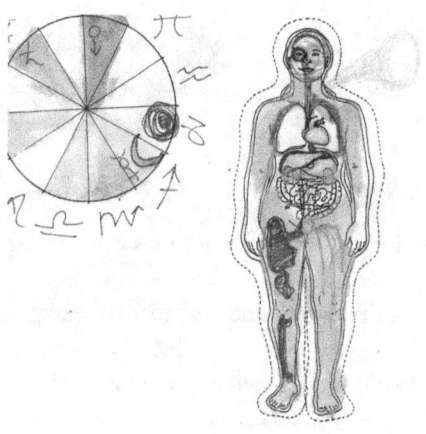

eMVI = electromagnetic vibrational imprint, page 1
A collaborative tool designed by Andrea Gehrz
& Casey Cardoso

One of the most healing uses of astrology is the examination of the chart through a bio-vibrational lens. Most people in modern society are familiar with the hippocratic oath. This is the oath taken by doctors, promising not to harm their patients. This oath was originally written circa 500 BC. The first natal chart discovered was found to have been calculated around 400 BC. At this time in history, the four humours were used in medicine and were also linked to the astrological chart. In fact, the hippocratic oath is at times thought to have been written by Pythagorus, who is closely linked to astrology. Pythagorus was well known for his ideas about reincarnation, planetary aspects, and the manner in which the aspects correlate to musical chords. The four humours in astrology are as follows:

Earth Black Bile   **Fire** Yellow Bile
Water Phlegm   **Air** Blood

Historically, illness was often thought to have been caused by an excess or deficiency of one of the humours. For instance, someone with too much fire in the chart was thought of as a "choleric" type of individual, while a person with too much earth was thought to be "melancholic." Too much water has been called "phlegmatic," while too much air is known to create a "sanguine" temperament. The four elements were also associated with certain qualities of air and temperature. Yellow bile was thought of as hot and dry, while phlegm was thought to be mucousy and cold like water. Black bile was cold and dry, while blood was thought to be hot and moist.

Black Bile Cold and Dry   **Yellow Bile** Hot and Dry
Phlegm Cold and Moist   **Blood** Hot and Moist

In ancient times, it was commonplace for physicians to prescribe a regimen of diet, exercise, and other activities in order to bring the humours into balance.

Whether or not the hippocratic oath was written by Hippocrates or Pythagorus is a moot point. What is interesting to notice is that Hippocrates lived during the same time period that astrology was emerging as a genethliological practice[9]. And we can easily see from the concept of the humours that astrology and the four elements were an integral part of medical treatment and diagnosis[10].

There have been many developments in the fields of both medical astrology and modern medicine, yet the parallel still remains. Both doctors and astrologers are meant and able to heal people. Medical astrology has advanced greatly through the practice and research performed by certain doctors, herbalists, etc., who are also astrologers. Some of my favorite books on medical astrology are as follows:

Encyclopedia of Medical Astrology, by H.L. Cornell

Medical Astrology: A Guide to Planetary Pathology,
by Judith Hill

Taber's Cyclopedic Medical Dictionary, by F.A. Davis

---

[9] Genethliology is a fancy word meaning, "*the use of astrology to study the lives of individual persons.*"

[10] For a more thorough discussion of this topic, read Deborah Houlding's phenomenal article in the February 2012 edition of *The Mountain Astrologer* entitled *Hippocrates, Humours, and Temperament in Traditional Astrology and Medicine.*

Medical Astrology: the Basics

The Planet represents the specific vibrations and influxes that will be affecting the energy field and physical body.

The Sign shows the area(s) of the body through and into which the planetary energies will flow.

Aries	Head/Brain
Taurus	Ears/Teeth/Jaw/Throat
Gemini	Throat/Arms/Lungs
Cancer	Pleura around the Lungs/Stomach
Leo	Back/Heart/Spine
Virgo	Pancreas/Intestines
Libra	Kidneys/Lower Back
Scorpio	Colon/Genitals/Nostrils
Sagittarius	Nerves in Hips/Butt/Thighs
Capricorn	Bones/Skin/Knees
Aquarius	Blood vessels/Ankles
Pisces	Feet/Lymph/Perineum[11]

---

[11] For a more extensive list of body parts, and a great description of how to approach the chart from a medical perspective, see Judith Hill's *Medical Astrology; A Guide of Planetary Pathology.* For the serious student, check out Cornell's *Encyclopedia of Medical Astrology.*

Planetary Correlations

The Sun: The vitality, physical constitution, immune function, and general vibrancy.

The Moon: The nourishment needs, appetites, manner of eating, and emotional constitution.

Mercury: The mental body, nervous system, synaptic activity, language function, and logic center.

Venus: The sweetness tendencies, glands and hormones that produce cravings for sugar.

Mars: The heat and inflammation tendencies, the glands and hormones that bring out aggression.

Saturn: The coldness and constriction tendencies, the glands and hormones that suppress function.

Jupiter: The growth and expansion tendencies, the glands and hormones that incite growth.

Uranus: The electrical system of the body, the glands and hormones that produce excitement.

Neptune: Subtle input and internal stimuli, the glands and hormones that produce sensitivity to vibration and light.

Pluto: The obsessive tendency, the glands and hormones that create dependancy and powerlessness.

Most physical health problems can be attributed to Saturn or Mars. Mars and Saturn could be said to be malevolent and malicious inasmuch as they tend to produce experiences that are physically or emotionally uncomfortable. In our modern culture, Mars afflictions are to be feared; fevers must be controlled, cuts are infections waiting to happen, and rashes are to be suppressed with creams. Saturn problems, such as constipation and low blood pressure, are also to be avoided.

It is important to understand that the other planets play a role in physical illness as well. Venus can be attributed to an excessive amount of sugar or sweetness in the system, while Jupiter can bring such great expansion as to create tumors, cysts, obesity, or even bunions. Uranus brings in electricity to the vibrational field, at times overexciting the system, causing synaptically interesting events to occur. Uranian problems can present as tourettes, seizures, narcolepsy, spasms, etc.

Neptune can be linked to various sorts of psychic problems such as mental illness, extreme co-dependence, and sleep disorders. In extreme cases, Pluto can produce intense terminal illnesses such as crohn's disease or gangrenous problems that might even lead to the amputation of a body part. As we can see, each and every planet can in fact cause physical illness in the body. This is because each planet has a vibrational quality that could potentially create an imbalance in the system.

The following pages show examples of health maladies caused by Mars and Saturn throughout the signs.

Example: Saturn brings in a cold, restrictive, tight, and necrotic energy. In the context of medical astrology, Saturn tends to produce constrictive problems, coldening and slowing problems, suppression, etc.

Sign Placement of Saturn	Energetic Quality of this Placement	Manifestation of Physical Illness
Saturn in Aries	Coldness in the Head Tightness in the Head	Ex: Constrictive Migraines
Saturn in Taurus	Tightening of the Teeth Coldness in the Ear	Ex: Receding gumline Clogged Ear
Saturn in Gemini	Tightness in the Lungs Constriction in the Arm	Ex: Cold-induced Asthma Constricted Tendon
Saturn in Cancer	Constricted Stomach	Ex: Suppressed Stomach Acids
Saturn in Leo	Cooled and Suppressed Heart	Ex: Low Blood Pressure
Saturn in Virgo	Cool and Constricted Intestines	Ex: Slow Peristalsis Constipation
Saturn in Libra	Constricted Kidneys	Ex: Suppressed Kidney Function Necrotic Kidneys
Saturn in Scorpio	Constricted Colon	Ex: Colonic Blockages

Example: Mars is an energy which is very hot. In the context of medical astrology, Mars tends to produce inflammatory problems and illnesses that are accompanied by a fever, heat rash, etc.

Sign Placement of Mars	Energetic Quality of this Placement	Manifestation of Physical Illness
Mars in Aries	Heat to the Head Heat to the Brain	Ex: Hot Migraines Hot Temper
Mars in Taurus	Heat to the Ears Heat to the Teeth Heat to the Throat	Ex: Tooth Infection Tonsillitis
Mars in Gemini	Heat to the Arms Heat in the Lungs	Ex: Tendonitis in the Arm Lung Infection
Mars in Cancer	Heat in the Stomach	Ex: Acid Reflux
Mars in Leo	Heat in the Heart Heat in the Spine	Ex: Ruptured Disk
Mars in Virgo	Heat in the Intestines	Ex: Inflamed Intestines
Mars in Libra	Heat in the Kidneys	Ex: Inflamed Kidneys
Mars in Scorpio	Heat in the Genitals	Ex: Herpes

9

Astrological Diagnosis[12]

---

[12] *Dia-Gnosis* = distinguishing, a means of distinguishing

from the Greek verb:

Dia-gnomeo = to consider, reflect, deliberate.

from the Greek roots

Dia = through, throughout.
in different directions.
to the end (of a matter), utterly.

&

Gnosis = a seeking to know. an inquiry. investigation
a knowledge of a thing, person, etc.

Isolating the problematic planet or aspect, is the first step in astrological diagnosis. Let us now set out an operational definition of *astrological diagnosis*.

Astrological Diagnosis

The act of identifying and naming an emotional, mental, physical, or behavioral problem through a description of the vibrational pattern that is underlying its manifestation.

When we go to the doctor with a problem, we expect to leave with the name of our problem, and a time frame in which we can expect the problem to go away. This is usually how things go at the doctor's office, and we often leave feeling a sense of relief. At times, however, there exist physical, emotional, or behavioral difficulties that seem to defy conventional treatment.

Allopathic doctors are experts in conventional treatment. The modern medical system is in fact an institution. Modern medical doctors must follow rules, prescribe certain agreed upon medications, and analyze numbers using standardized methods of measurement. Modern doctors hold a very concrete and specific role in our society. Western doctors are marvelous remediators of concrete, saturnian problems.

Many illnesses are in fact saturnian in nature, but we want to use caution not to communicate information to clients in a saturnian way. Certain diagnoses can in fact produce a great deal of fear, helplessness and dread. What we are primarily talking about here is the diagnosis of illnesses that are not saturnian in nature. Oftentimes, a concrete diagnosis will be made for an illness that is lacking in concrete structure.

When a person breaks a bone, this is in fact a concrete ailment. The body has been compromised through a crack in its very structure. Often, doctors will put in metal pins, screws, or some other sort of hard material in order to repair the structural damage that has occurred. This is a wonderful use of Saturn; to recreate a new and better structure.

While two people can break their arm, and each break will be different in nature, the procedure and healing method will be more similar than different. In each of the two broken bone cases, there will indeed be a process of rebuilding the structure of the bone. The exact process of how that bone will be set must of course be tailored to the specific bone that has been broken.

Now let us look at some more subjective illnesses, such as schizophrenia, certain types of cancer, fibromyalgia, candida syndrome, etc. When we say a more "subjective illness" here, we are meaning that each individual who might have one of the aforementioned illnesses will experience that illness differently than each other person who has had that illness. There are a number of diseases which could be said to be more neptunian in nature. These are the more vague and energetically depleting kinds of illnesses such as systemic illness, lymphatic illness, glandular disturbances, mental illnesses, rashes, hormonal problems, hypoglycemia, adrenal fatigue, etc.

In modern allopathic medical practices, certain emotional problems can develop when a neptunian illness is given a saturnian diagnosis or label. A western doctor may use language such as:

Ma'am, you have systemic leukemia and may only have three months left to live.

Your previously unexplained rash is psoriasis. You will have it forever. Psoriasis is a lifelong problem.

You have a rare form of multiple sclerosis.. You will never again be able to walk.

In cases such as these, astrological diagnosis can be very healing and helpful. Mental illnesses are perfect candidates for astrological diagnosis, for the simple reason that each and every person's experience of mental illness is entirely unique.

During my years as a sign language interpreter, I have interpreted many classes on abnormal psychology. Diagnostic labeling of mental illness is a highly simplified way of describing a person's experience of their own mental state. When a mental health specialist ascribes the diagnosis of bi-polar disorder to an individual, it could be said that one bi-polar person's experience of that problem is entirely different than the next person's. While two bi-polar people can in fact bond over their common diagnosis and symptoms, they might not be able to bond over a common *perceptive* experience at all.

The act of modern diagnosis is very saturnian because of the fact that Saturn rules structures and institutions. Diagnosing illnesses helps people get services and treatment. A diagnosis of bi-polar disorder can help a person be understood by institutions and other structures, so that the individual can get his or her basic needs met. This would of course be in the case that the mental illness had begun to affect and collapse the structures of the person's life. In this way, the labeling and diagnosis of people can be healing. If we are to heal illnesses that are energetic, emotional, or spiritual in nature however, we must attack the problem in an appropriate fashion. We must attempt to heal the energy-body.

This could look as simple as believing the things that the mentally ill person is saying are true, or as complex as performing an exorcism. The necessary treatment depends upon the entire astrological makeup and the vibrations that are influxing into the person at the current time. Regardless of the treatment necessary, a useful first step is to clarify and ascribe language to the planets that have been causing the problematic emotions, experiences, and behaviors. Let us now examine the process of astrological diagnosis through the use of a few examples.

Example One: Astrological Diagnosis

Physical and emotional symptoms of imbalance: Inability to keep a job, intense emotional ups and downs, fixation on certain explosive art projects, excessive talking which then leads to extreme agitation and reclusive tendencies.

Allopathic Diagnosis: Manic Depressive.

Natal configuration causing the problem:

> Sun/Mercury/Mars conjunction at 4-6 Aries, *opposite* to Uranus at 9 Libra.

Questions that could lead us to a diagnosis of what is occurring within the energy-body:

What is the exact nature of the energetic flow? Is the person's tendency to be hot then cold, or cold then hot? Is there a physical-vibrational component? Is Mercury involved? How many degrees are separating the energies in the aspect? Is there a tendency to be violent or self-harming? When did the problem begin? In general, are depressive episodes connected to lost relationships? Is the depression more boredom-induced or blockage-induced? Is the person generally pent up or overly expressive? Is Uranus causing the problem? Is the problem erratic or is it cyclical? Is the problem natal or transiting?

Analysis: The client gets extreme influxings of seemingly uncontrollable talkative energies, on account of Mercury sitting with Mars and the Sun in Aries. The person identifies very much with their hot-tempered personality, as Aries is upon the Ascendant as well. When transiting energies ignite this part of the chart, the energy flows to extremes. The keyed up and hot energies lead to seemingly unexpected separations with people on account of Uranus in Libra in the seventh house. The problem has been present since childhood. The depression is primarily focused on relationship difficulties that are a direct result of the extreme nature of the verbal tendency.

Astrological Diagnosis: Astro-congenital heat build up in the head and throat area leads to impulsive behaviors such as non-stop talking, poor impulse control, and a hot temper. These behaviors then cause unexpected separative tendencies in relationships of all kinds. The separations lead to sadness over what has been lost. The problem is natal in nature and will thus need to be dealt with on a long term basis.

Example Two: Astrological Diagnosis

Physical and emotional symptoms of imbalance: Fatigue, feeling constantly lackluster, extreme apathy, boredom, an exceptionally hard time dealing with details; cleanliness, dressing the self well, and exact routines, etc.

Allopathic Diagnosis: Chronic Fatigue Syndrome

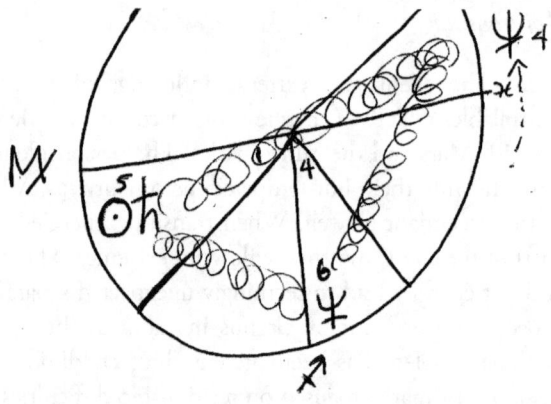

Natal configuration causing the problem:

> Sun/Saturn conjunction at 5 degrees *square* to natal Neptune at 6 Sagittarius.

Transit exacerbating the problem:

> Traveling Neptune *opposing* natal Sun/Saturn, and *squaring* natal Neptune.

Questions that could lead us to a diagnosis of what is occurring within the energy-body:

What is the exact planetary nature of the fatigue? Is the fatigue constant, cyclical, or intermittent? Has fatigue been a lifelong problem or is it new? Is there a mineral deficiency? Is there a tendency to be depressive or energetically overwhelmed? Does the person clear lymph fluid easily? Is the problem occurring erratically?

Analysis: The chart shows a natal tendency towards fatigue, as the Sun is sitting under the cold and constrictive rays of Saturn. This can cool down the chi force, creating a slow, steady emission of the thermal and metabolic energies. The Sun and Saturn in Virgo could bring some of the constrictive energies to the intestines, perhaps slowing down the intestinal rhythm, leading to slow peristalsis and fatigue. Also, the square to natal Neptune exacerbates the problem by introducing dissolution to the structure-producing tendencies of Saturn. While the native is generally low energy, the problem is being greatly worsened by transiting Neptune adding to the slow, foggy energies.

Astrological Diagnosis: Astro-congenital tendency towards energetic and structural weakness on account of the Sun, Saturn, and Neptune. Weakness is causing problems with the intestinal health, as well as the nervous system in general (natal Neptune in Sagittarius). Problem is natal, with exacerbation by current transits. Healing modalities must be ongoing, with an initial focus on introducing good bacteria into the digestive tract.

10

Isolating the Planets that Need Remediation

There are a number of ways to isolate a problematic planet or aspect-cluster. When performing astrological analysis, diagnosis, and suggesting remedial options, it is crucial to make sure that we are aware of all of the planets potentially causing the symptoms. Without this information, we are just "shooting in the dark," as they say. Whether the problem is physical, emotional, or mental in nature, the approach used to locate the problematic planet or configuration will be similar. Often times, the astral hardship is exceedingly obvious. If the struggle is in relation to love or creativity and we see Saturn sitting upon Venus, then we know we have found our culprit.

If person is experiencing lower back pain and we find Saturn sitting upon Mars in Libra, then we will know that the symbology matches exactly with the chart (Libra rules the lower back). If we are easily able to locate the transit on which the suffering began, we can then work to find useful remediations for all of the planets involved in the configuration. We will want to remediate for the entire duration of the transit, as the vibrations will be influxing into the field until the end of this time period.

One of the first methods we will use to identify the source of a problem is to look into the past to locate the exact time when the symptoms began. If the transits do not clearly indicate the source of the illness, a progression can at times be the culprit. When it becomes obvious that a progression is indeed causing certain symptoms, then we will also need to address such problematic vibrations for the entire duration of the progression[13].

At times, a person will have a natal aspect that causes ongoing problems. In this case, we will want to isolate the aspect and begin to invent possible remediations. We can then anticipate transits and progressions to the natal configuration in order to soothe the soul during these time periods. It can occur that a progressed planet might station in such a way that it creates long-lasting problems. We will need to remediate these planets

---

[13] Most often an allopathic diagnosis will come near the middle to end of a stressful transit, as the new influxings of vibrations and thoughts tend to take us by surprise. It often takes us a while to realize that the problem will continue. When we notice that the problem is not getting better, we seek outside assistance. Moreover, the ending of a health transit can at times be marked by a modern remedial measure that fixes the problem, such as a pill, surgery, etc.

for the long term; almost as if the configuration were to exist in the natal chart. If neither the current transits nor progressions indicate any concern, then a bit of detective work will be necessary in order to isolate problematic energies.

There are two components to this process. The first possible option is to ask the client to keep a record of flare ups of the problem, their exact timing, and the symptomology of each incident. If the problem is affecting the physical health, then the client can record days on which the pain or discomfort is at its worst. At times, the suffering will be emotional. In these cases, the client will need to document days that are marked by internal strife.

A second method to locate the energies is to look into the ephemeris to time upcoming transits from the inner planets to the problematic configuration. If a person is having a problem with the deterioration of a certain part of the body, we might look to Neptune. If we are unclear as to whether the problem is with natal or transiting Neptune, then we can simply time and observe some transits from the inner planets, to both. We will also want to make sure that the transiting Moon is also there to trigger the aspect.

Many years ago, I encountered a client with a most bizarre health problem; a burning back and shoulders. During certain time periods, this particular client would have an extremely, intense burning sensation in her shoulders. The problem was so disruptive that she was unable to lay on her back, her work life was interrupted, etc. The situation was dire. A glance at the chart showed the problematic planets almost immediately.

Symptomology:

Physical: High levels of testosterone production. Testosterone surges that cause cyclical and intense excitement and surgings of heat. Burning shoulders. Severe and debilitating.

Emotional: The desire and longing to have fun to the maximum degree. High levels of empassionment.

Behavioral: Recklessness. Extreme excitement. A frequent need to let loose through the art of extreme adventure. A love of passionate music and all things daring and fun.

Mental: Frustration at inability to figure out what is causing the shoulder inflammation. Thoughts that it would be best if the native was made differently. Hopelessness.

A little sleuthing and we find our culprit:

"North Node in Leo conjunct to Mars brings about abundant energy, strong muscles, athleticism, excess of testosterone or adrenaline. May run high fevers. Take care in the case of overheating, overexertion, strokes, etc. Successful for all Mars careers."

Medical Astrology: A Guide to Pathology, by Judith Hill page 67

Problematic Conjunction: *Located*

Mars at 3 Leo
North Node at 1 Leo

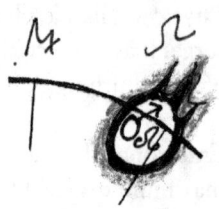

On the day of this woman's birth, the hot planet of Mars had been sitting in Leo, *conjunct* to the North Node of the Moon. Medically and emotionally speaking, the North Node will magnify and multiply the energy of any planet upon that Node. In general, Mars energies will manifest through physical symptoms. The likelihood of this aspect being the symptom-maker was increased by Mars being situated in a fire sign of Leo, as this indicates even more heat coming into the body through the back and shoulder area.

When we see a planet or aspect that we think is the cause of suffering, we can take our inquiry a step further by looking into exact timing. This act will often give us a confirmation that we have indeed done our thought-work correctly. In the case of the girl with the burning shoulders, her Mars/North Node conjunction was also situated in an exact square aspect to Uranus in Scorpio, in her ninth house. I asked her if the shoulder flare ups tended to occur while traveling. She responded that this was in fact her experience. In order to get a confirmation, I then got out my ephemeris to time some possible past incidences of shoulder inflammation. This way, I could be sure that I had located the correct configuration. We were then easily able to match up her problem with the most recent Saturn transit to the hot aspect. We also looked at just a few weeks earlier when transiting Mars had hit the aspect and this also coincided with an intensely inflamed shoulder. Once the aspect had been confirmed, we then began an attempt at remediating the problem.

If I were to attempt to remediate this same problem today, I would try both a cooling remedy as well as an outlet for the intense heat of the aspect. I would also recommend that this girl avoid spicy foods and being in the Sun for excessive periods of time on heat-inducing transits to the Mars/North Node conjunction. (A common problem is that her body cannot cool itself down on account of the Mars/North Node.) I would also prescribe an outlet to release the martian energy, such as body-building with a focus on the shoulders, or acupuncture if the heat was somehow blocked up. If we were not able to easily locate the natal aspect that was causing the burning shoulders, we could ask the client to track future flare-ups. We could then compare the client's notes to the transit activity.

Now that we understand a bit about the definition and uses of astrological remediation, we can continue our journey into the technical apparatus of the study. We begin the next section by developing a thorough understanding of the qualities and vibrations of the planets, and the effects of these emissions on our minds, bodies, and souls. We will then build up to an understanding of the manner in which to synthesize the planetary vibrations with the sign and house in which they are sitting. From there, we will take a look at the behavior of natal aspects, in preparation to begin the art of remediating any possible configuration we might encounter.

Remedial Schematica

11

The Planets in Remediation

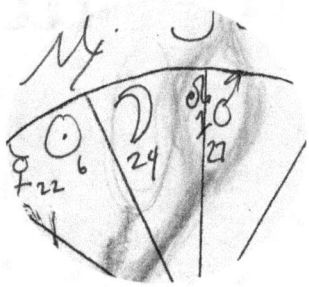

The planets can be thought of as
the "energy-producers" within the astral schematic.

Through their various emissive qualities,
the planets incite facets of the life experience.

11.1 The Sun

Sun vibrations: Brightness, vibrancy, enlivenment, existence, engagement of the senses, awakening, incitement, photonic activation, and light.

Sun needs: The need to exist, be recognized, form an identity, move the body, feed the body through activity, be productive and practical, shine, form an outer-identification, and engage the senses.

People who represent the Sun: Characters, entrepreneurs, people that everyone knows, people who get recognized, people of ranking, figureheads, spokespeople, celebrities.

Problematic presentations of the Sun: Narcissism, self-aggrandizement, an overabundance of self-focused energies, being painfully shy or reclusive, inability to dress the self well, self-deprecating behaviors, worry over the identity, lack of vibrance, challenges involving the sensory or perceptive faculties.

Sun remediations for physical health and well-being: Activities that care for the physical body, massages, rubbing, exercising, moving one's body, being touched by someone who loves our body, getting enough Sun and light, cleansing or cleaning the physical body, getting a physical exam.

Sun remediations for emotional health and well-being: Dressing the physical body well, recognizing and defining one's own identity, focusing on the practical needs of the life, being in the Sun, integrating various parts of oneself, keeping well-groomed and bathed.

The Sun could be said to rule the vital energy within us. Each human being is composed of billions of cells, all busy going through thermal, enzymatic, and dynamic processes. These processes are controlled by the glands, hormones, and sugars within the bloodstream, which are controlled by the brain. When we open our eyes and take in photonic particles from the Sun, we are enlivened as our cells begin to convert sugar to energy. The state of our whole perception of being is connected with the Sun, including the physical, sensory, and perceptive experience.

When the Sun is maltreated in the chart, we will want to attack the problem through a multi-layered approach, attending to the blood, endocrine system, nerves, heart, brain, glands, and spinal cord. The best approach is to attend to the whole being; mind, body, and spirit.

On an inner level, the Sun is connected to our need to be recognized as a distinct and identified individual. If the Sun is highly maltreated in a natal chart, a person with such a configuration may feel that they must struggle to be who they are. Sun malaise can manifest as a wrangling with one's identity, feelings of being invisible, struggling to get the most basic needs met, etc. The Sun is what drives the part of us that is unique to only us. In adults, a time that is heavily Sun-laden might be when a person decides to brand their business, become more precise about the manner in which to dress and clothe the physical body, or to get physical needs met. The identity in the outer sphere may also be affected.

Each person will experience an influxing of energy to their Sun each year on their birthday. On this very special day, the traveling Sun returns to the place where it sat in the cosmos on the day of our birth. It is on this day that we get to celebrate our own place in the world and the fact that we exist. Persons with a malaised Sun will feel left out and lonely on their birthday, whereas happy Sun people will joyfully celebrate their existence with friends and family. Persons with a hard Sun configuration will need extra love and support on the day of their birth, as they might feel that their role in the world is unimportant or inconsequential. Remediations for Sun problems can often include focus, attention, and love given to the identity and person in general. Physical remediations shall focus on the entire body and vitality, as well as the part of the body indicated by the sign in which the Sun is sitting at birth.

11.2 The Moon

Moon vibrations: Effluxive, influxive, essential, nourishing of the soul-spirit, alivening of the inner senses, emotional, morphing, pulling, pushing, urging, and constant.

Moon needs: The need to exist inwardly, be emotional, be nourished, feed and care for the soul, caretake, be emotionally fulfilled, satisfy the appetite, engage the process of inner-identification, and reflect.

People who represent the Moon: Caretakers, nannies, bed and breakfast owners, cooks, mothers, psychologists, architects, chefs, hotel owners, bakers.

Problematic presentations of the Moon: Constant crying, overprotectiveness, smothering emotions, imbalance in emotional partnerships, chaotic or conflicted home life, emotional volatility, dietary issues, eating disorders, not listening to or expressing the internal sphere.

Moon remediations for physical health and well-being: Dietary management, making the home healthy, getting feelings out, eating the highest version of what the body craves, being mothered in regards to the health, finding physical activities that match the emotional needs, eating miracle foods (avocados, miso, coconut, fermented foods, ghee).

Moon remediations for emotional health and well-being: Manifesting uplifting emotional relationships, going out to eat at nice restaurants, snuggling, hugging, holding, crying, caretaking others, cooking for people, telling people we love them, expressing emotions through methods that work best according to the sign of the Moon, connecting with family, cleaning the kitchen.

The Moon is connected to the fluids inside the body and the internal sphere. As the Moon pulls on the tides, she also affects our emotional needs by tugging at our heartstrings. In some ways, the Moon can also be thought of as representing the home and entire family, for the place in which we do most of our emoting and eating is generally at home. One way to remediate a Moon problem is through the use of food, but nurturing of all kinds can be involved. Remedial measures for the Moon might also have something to do with the home, as getting the appetites balanced depends a great deal on the calmness of the home life.

We can always attack a Moon problem from the inside, by providing food options to balance out the needs the chart. Because each person has their own unique appetites, we must do so by attending to the sign placement and configuration of the Moon.

The twelve love languages and internal appetites as indicated by the sign of the Moon

Aries: Feisty and reckless adoration. The need for emotional and sensual adventures and bold expression. The need to "go off." Love as passion and fierceness. Love as heat. Appetite as adventure.

Taurus: Love as stability, patience, and emotional foundation building. Appetites as calm and consistent. Love as resource providing and enduring.

Gemini: A need for emotional variety and emotional change. Emotions as a verbal expression. Emotions as words. Emotions as ideas. Appetites as reinvention and evolving logic.

Cancer: Love as nurturing, cooking, care taking, and homemaking. The need to tend to others. Love as home. The need to please the appetite through careful nourishing.

Leo: Love as adoration, beauty, and being enlivened. Love as words of affirmation. Appetites as a vehicle for fun. The need to be internally recognized and made to feel special.

Virgo: Love as acts of service and detail-oriented care. Attending to specific and particular needs. The need to be of assistance.

Libra: Love as connection, communion, and quality time. The need to become one. The need to discover, relate to, and share beauty. The appetites as they are incited by sharing. Love as art.

Scorpio: Love as intense connection. Emotional depth. Loyalty and passion. The appetites as intense feeling-based waves. The need to find beauty in depth. The need to be transformed through love.

Sagittarius: Love through optimism, joy, and faith-bringing. Love as an act of creating joy. Love as freedom. Love as expansion. Satisfying the appetites through travel and movement. The need for positivity.

Capricorn: Love as emotional structuring, boundary-making, and endurance. The need for high-level structure. Love as an institution. The need for ranking within love. The need to be respected.

Aquarius: Friendship as love. Love of the group. The appetites as a form of community connection and social change. Love as a sociological institution. Love as community activism. Love as politics.

Pisces: Love as transcendence. The appetites as a vehicle for divine expression. Idealistic love. Love without boundaries. Love as special and non-earthly. Love as separate from the body.

When we are examining problems of the Moon it is important to look to the diet and the appetites, to see how these parts of life might somehow be linked to any emotional suffering. An undernourished appetite can lead to an undernourished soul. The appetite begins with salt, the ancient flavor attributed to the Moon. Salt is important in that it brings out all other flavors. It is also used to ferment foods. Fermented foods, which are not pasteurized, can in fact heal many other processes in the body, as cells need enzymes in order for cell-reactions to take place. The internal needs of each and every person are entirely unique. The style in which a person feels best nourished can be understood by the sign of the Moon in the natal chart. In total, the sign, house placement, and aspects to the Moon will indicate our peculiar internal experience as it is represented by the celestial sphere at birth[14].

For example, a person with a natal Moon/Saturn aspect might have a tendency to be very food-restrictive. Saturn can block the flow of energy and heat coming to or from a certain part of the life experience. When the traveling planets light up the Moon/Saturn aspect, the individual might feel very averse to consuming food at all, because the internal appetite is being constricted by Saturn. With a chart such as this, it might be important to alert the client of times during which he or she might be feeling especially constrictive, so that a plan can be made to consume nutrient rich foods that are also not too expansive, nor require too much energy to burn. At first, a

---

[14] If you are new to astrology, you may want to jump ahead and read the chapter on *aspects*, as the angles between the planets will be mentioned throughout the next sections. A simple understanding of the planetary symbols and aspects can make a chart come alive!

person with such a configuration might want to simplify the diet. He or she may like to cook recipes that have already been developed, or eating traditional foods, as the food structure is already set. Eating a kosher diet might be very soothing in this case.

After the client is in control of his or her diet, it is time for the Moon/Saturn individual to build up their own unique appetite structure. The chart-holder must ultimately decide which foods sit well with the constrictive stomach. Another effect Saturn can have upon the Moon is to make most food seem unappealing. The best remediation for this might be to work hard at cooking food that tastes delicious. Perfecting a recipe or creating one's own traditional foods is a great way to satisfy this energy.

A person with a Moon/Jupiter conjunction will have a very different internal experience. A Moon/Jupiter person may have an expansive appetite and a tendency to over-eat. I have witnessed a child with a Moon/Jupiter conjunction go on "eating spurts" like clockwork, when planets such as Venus or the Sun activate the configuration. This is a good thing because children are made to grow! With an internally-expansive child, a balancing technique will also be helpful. For instance, we could teach the concept of "portion control" to the child, but only when the time is appropriate, such as when Saturn is hitting the conjunction. At this point, Saturn would be acting to cool off the appetites a bit, and the child would be able to accept lessons of control and restraint.

Sun conjunct Moon aspects often indicate that the internal appetites and the physical body are inherently connected. It will be important to nourish both the outer Sun-self and the internal Moon-self, as they will be entirely connected to one another.

A Moon/Venus connection might bring an excessive liking of sugar. Now suppose a client arrives in our office with a Moon/Venus conjunction in Scorpio. She cannot stop craving and obsessing over sugar. Sugar is a venusian food and a universal connector. If an adult is wanting to win over a child's attention, they will often provide sweet treats and candy. The underlying energy here is the need for communing, connection, and commonality. Sweetness. Everything that makes life worth living.

One thing we can do to remediate an overactive Venus/Moon aspect is to give Venus more energetically pure forms of sugar. Cookies that are made from scratch with love are very different than cookies bought in a package. The former could be understood as an authentic experience of sweetness and love, while the latter might seem like a cheap substitute for the real thing.

One method of food remediation would be to direct the client to eat a variety of healthy venusian foods. Some examples are dates, raisins, fruit, homemade pies, etc. Another way to remediate would be to socialize while eating. Throwing a dinner party, or making sweets for other people can facilitate getting these needs met.

The ability of a Moon/Mercury person to eat will have much to do with their mental state. Because Mercury rules the mind, Moon/Mercury people tend to naturally engage the mind and the internal appetites at the same time. If the person is having a hard time eating on account of anxiety or mental instability, it may be important to be able to read or talk while eating. If there is no one with which to converse, it may be helpful to watch TV, do mind puzzles, or listen to talk radio. It is also important to provide these clients with a vast array of food-language, as this will add to the mental experience of eating.

Moon/Mars contacts create emotional heat. People with this configuration tend to crave hot foods and emotional intensity. One way to antidote this is to have them eat cold foods such as ice cream, ice chips, watermelon, etc. It is also important to make sure that these persons get enough protein. Another method is to give a Moon/Mars person pickled foods, which are *pikros*[15], meaning that the flavor is exciting and sharp; the kind of foods that "pack a punch," yet can be cooling in their effect.

If a person has a Uranus/Moon contact, they will inhabit a constantly changing and vivacious appetite. This aspect can present as a need for evolution of the emotional appetites. The best way to remediate a Moon/Uranus is to constantly innovate the diet with new and exciting ingredients. For a person such as this, appetite equals freedom. Being able to choose what to eat and having new foods is crucial for the emotional health and well-being of the Moon/Uranus individual. Books such as *The Improvisational Cook* or *Think Like a Chef* are great for clients with Uranus touching their Moon. Another method could be to to explore ethnic cooking which introduces new ingredients to the diet.

---

[15] See chapter 25 for more info on *pikros*.

Moon/Pluto problems can create situations of internal dependency. The appetites and emotional nature might be quite potent and intense, as the internally reflected light of the Moon at birth would have been given a laser-like, fixative feel by being in contact with Pluto. Some remediations for a Moon/Pluto contact could be as extreme as surgical restructuring of the physical body, alteration of the DNA, or exorcisms.

11.3 MERCURY

Mercury vibrations: Fast, active, cerebral, synaptic, lingual, cognitive, perceptive, integrative, processive, frenetic, expressive, narrative-building, filtering, and disclosive.

Mercury needs: The need to express the urges, integrate information, share meaning, process information, perceive the world, be cognitive, translate thought-pictures into language, create a mental framework, disclose one's experience, and understand the perceptive experiences of others.

People who represent Mercury: Interpreters, auctioneers, teachers, writers, radio personalities, news anchors, public speakers, scholars, commentators, mediators, journalists.

Problematic presentations of Mercury: Over-talking, frequent use of social media, under-talking or being painfully shy, not being able to communicate, language disorders, dyslexia, lack of appropriate vocabulary for the internal experience, being overly brash, mumbling, sore throats, speech struggles, morbid thinking, obsessive thinking, overly defensive thinking, being verbally caustic, the inability to be verbally kind, swearing and being foul, not being able to express oneself, feeling alienated.

Mercury remediations for physical health and well-being: Eating nutritious foods that give energy to the mind, balancing the blood sugar so that the mind is not functioning with depleted energy, walking or moving to introduce new stimuli, learning through conversation, speaking about mental pictures of the body being healthy, using vitamins that help the mind function well, hypnosis into more healthy thought forms.

Mercury remediations for emotional health and well-being: Talking about one's problems, writing, creating happy thought structures, ridding the soul of thoughts that cause cognitive dissonance[16], giving and receiving positive affirmation, reading, journaling, taking control of one's own paradigm, connecting through social media, studying, taking a writing class, writing a manifesto to purge hard narratives, writing an integrated and holistic narrative.

Mercury can produce problematic thinking or communication when it is highly maltreated. The main struggle with a maltreated Mercury is that there exists a challenge in communicating the needs and intentions of the remaining

---

[16] **Cognitive Dissonance:** The holding of two or more incompatible attitudes or beliefs in one's mental framework at the same time. Such as in, *smokers are bad people* and *I am a smoker*. These two thoughts being given value simultaneously will create suffering the mind of the person thinking them.

planets in the chart. While it is indeed possible to meet one's own needs, this is never true in all cases. For example, children depend on their parents to meet certain needs. We have all witnessed pre-lingual children crying with frustration at not being able to express their inner desires.

Mercury is the planet of perception and communication. The sign in which Mercury is placed will be indicative of the style of learning. When dealing with a problematic Mercury, it is very important that the learning style and communication patterns be honored. For some individuals, the perfect style of learning is haphazard and erratic. Another might crave silence, such as a child who prefers to learn through quiet reading.

Certain charts have a Mercury that seeks to connect, while others have a mind that intends to separate and notice distinctions. At times, the modern medical model of handling intense Mercury variations is to label kids and adults with disorders such as:

ADD - Mercury square Uranus
Dyslexia - Mercury conjunct South Node
Learning disorders - Mercury conjunct/square Saturn
Autism - Mercury in Taurus, square Neptune
Oppositional Defiance Disorder - Mercury opposed Mars

A hard Mercury must be treated with care so as to not hamper a person's ability to fulfill the needs of the remaining planets[17].

Now let us use a fictional example of a teenager with a highly maltreated Mercury. Suppose that the student is very bright but can not easily talk on account of a severely malformed tongue. An astrologer could look into the chart to know where to start a conversation. Suppose we are to see Jupiter traveling through the student's natal 11th house in a very lucky position.

---

[17] In ancient astrology, the astrologers write often of
Planetary Classification:

Diurnal Class: *(Sun, Jupiter, Saturn)* = The practical and business needs.

Nocturnal Class: *(Moon, Venus, Mars)* = The internal nourishment needs.

Mercury is common to both classifications;
he processes internal experience and makes language.

Astrologer:

It looks like you have been making some friends recently.

Non-Lingual Teenager:

Shakes head No.

Have you recently had an opportunity come to you through a group or organization?

Nods happily.

Are you going to do something sweet, pleasant, exciting or fun in a group next week?

Nods happily. Eyes light up.

Can you use your communication board to tell me what you are doing?

Spells out, "Make a Wish Foundation is sponsoring me to get a makeover."

That sounds like fun! Everyone will most surely be touched by meeting you and seeing your evolution!

This example is fiction but I do often marvel at the possible uses of astrology to help non-lingual individuals. An interpreter can be quite effective at lightening feelings of distance and sadness in people who are communicatively impaired. For instance, if a person has a Mercury/Saturn conjunction and is cut off from communicating, it might be a refreshing treat to be able to have an in depth and meaningful conversation by answering a thousand yes or no questions.

It can be hard to generalize the manner in which to remediate for Mercury, as each person thinks so differently. When providing one's Mercury with an outlet for emotional happiness, the most important thing is to make sure that the person finds a way to express the internal self that is successful and in accordance with the natural tendencies of that individual.

A happy Mercury needs very little fixing, as the tendency will be towards positive thinking, acceptance, and mental expansion. A Mercury/Jupiter person can easily find humor in life. A person with a natal Mercury/Jupiter will easily integrate new parts of the self, as the narrative tends easily towards joy. This is also true in the case of a Mercury/Uranus. Both types of minds will be optimistic in their need to voraciously learn and open up, easily finding connections between new and past information. A well-situated Mercury gracefully builds upon existing knowledge.

A Mercury/Uranus individual can often learn best through invention. This is a happy Mercury, though it does not naturally play by the rules. A Mercury/Uranus conjunction is better suited for innovation, new thought-form production, and revolutionary ideas. A child with a peacefully eclectic mind might learn best by creating stories about the knowledge being learned. These children are well suited for harmonious innovation.

The more erratic and electric mind of a person with a Mercury/Uranus square can be a bit harder to reign in, as this mind has the potential to move extremely fast. These minds also seek to synthesize information through all sorts of uncommon methods, such as making up new words, thought forms, etc. A child with a highly inventive mind might learn to read by using cards with letters assigned to colors, pictures, and shapes. A child such as this might even all of a sudden seem to develop the ability to read in a single day.

I remember a time when I interpreted for a rowdy and eccentric, beautiful, butch comedian. Afterwards, I went home and looked up her chart. She kept saying things that surprised me! When I saw that she had an exact Mercury square Uranus, I was ironically not surprised. As a performer, she is very outspoken, funny and in your face. This is the exact nature of a Mercury square Uranus. It is not necessarily true that a person with this kind of Mercury cannot focus, but the focus will usually be upon making up new ideas. A mind such as this does not have much patience, as its role is to innovate ideas, make new mental pathways, and create new mental maps of the universe. Learning how to read is only a tiny step within this process. It can be tiring for a parent to keep up with or understand the erratic learning needs of a child with this configuration. As an astrologer, this is easily done by timing transits to the Mercury/Uranus square, as these will be highly teachable moments. The parent of a Mercury/Uranus child can enjoy the fact that these minds are quite attuned to finding anything they do to be interesting or exciting.

Teaching a Mercury/Uranus child while simultaneously moving the body through walking, playing, jumping, can be very effective. Often, children with inventive minds will not be able to relax enough to focus unless they are also being wrangled, stretched, spun, or pushed in a stroller. It might even work to teach them how to read while they themselves jump on a trampoline. This can bring a bit more focus to the mind, inasmuch as there is an inherent quality of chaos in the bodily movements.

Now let's take a look at a very different energy. An individual with a Mercury/Saturn connection will have a mind that is apt for creating mental structures. It will also find comfort in listening intently to structured thinking. A Mercury/Saturn individual adheres quite closely to facts and shared realities. This type of Mercury configuration can drive a person to continually judge him or herself against the standards of others. The challenge with a Mercury/Saturn is that it can lend itself too hyper-patterning. This can make it hard for a Mercury/Saturn individual to accept change and integrate new ideas.

Unexpected changes in plans can throw a Mercury/Saturn individual into a state of anxiety, as this mind seeks to create and adhere to structures and values integrity in regards to time. When two people make a plan, a mental structure has been created. In this case, the change in plans actually breaks the mental structure of the day's happenings.

If a person were to have a Mercury/Saturn conjunction, the outlook on life might be consistently serious, focused on negative thoughts, or oppressed in some way. For mental healing to occur, the first concept that must be taught to the Mercury/Saturn individual is that he or she is allowed to create original concepts. Oftentimes, when there is a Mercury/Saturn connection, the person continually waits for other people to feed him ideas, inwardly wanting to be told how to translate feelings into language. Mercury/Saturn individuals can often feel oppressed under their own constrictive thinking, and tend to easily submit to other people's ideas about who they are and how they should be.

A Mercury/Saturn child would be the type to remember and recite passages of books. Patterns and memorization feed a mind such as this, making it a good match for practicing rudiments, musical scales, grammar, reading, writing, or algebra. These activities healthily fulfill the need for expectations and the understanding of structures. They are simple and innocent modalities for practicing ideas of right and wrong, correct vs. incorrect, etc. A mind such as this could be funneled into patterned activities that are fitting to the entire chart, which could be anything from a sudoku puzzle to applied engineering.

A Mercury square Jupiter person will require a very different method of learning, as the challenge will lie in wanting to learn a great many things all at once. There might also be an inability to focus the mind to do the sustained work learning requires. A child with a Mercury square Jupiter might be caught fabricating ideas and lies, only because at times he will be overwhelmed by an intense need to buoyantly express himself. This kid will learn best through humor, joy and fun. In fact, there is nothing worse for a Mercury/Jupiter mind than to be expected to be overly serious and rigid. If forced to sit and listen for long periods of time, the need to have joyful and buoyant communication will come pouring out in other ways. Perhaps there will be notes doodled or laughing attacks.

A child such as this would love to learn complex concepts through fun and funny methods, not forcing a constriction, but instead opening up the mind to learn with as much enthusiasm as possible.

One way to heal and build up any Mercury is to speak to the highest in the chart. This technique inherently creates the most joyful and integrated narrative possible. The first step in creating a new story about one's life is to release old thoughts and ideas. This could be as simple as asking whether or not the person has been diagnosed with a disorder such as depression or bipolar mania, and then explaining the exact nature of the energies contributing to the label or diagnosis. This process presents new, nonjudgmental ideas that can be integrated with past diagnoses.

Another way to build up a person's mind is through positive affirmation. This is the simple technique of speaking to everything a person is doing well. If our client is using a certain energy in an interesting or positive way, we can mention and acknowledge this fact. We can also speak to the highest uses of any astrological signs that are prominent in the chart. A person might be greatly helped by being guided into creating a better story of his or her future. The manner through which to heal and help in the case of a problematic Mercury are endless. The main thing to remember is that Mercury is the catalyst through which we get the remainder of our planetary needs met. It is important that we understand the unique ways in which we integrate information, so that we can thrive within ourselves and among those around us.

11.4 Venus

Venus vibrations: Sweetening, loving, creationary, beauty-bringing, communal, connective, softening, pleasure-bringing, impassioning, uplifting, and pulsing.

Venus needs: The need to commune, connect, bond, be appealing, exchange sweetness and adoration, and emit beauty.

People who represent Venus: Musicians, artists, socialites, beauticians, designers, activity coordinators, candy makers, singers, bakers, lovers.

Problematic presentations of Venus: Expressing romantic love in ways that cause sorrow, being cold in one's expression of love, feeling as if there is no sweetness in life, over-indulgence in the sweetness of life, being overly effusive or obsequious, eating large amounts of refined sugar, hypoglycemia or hyperglycemia, blood sugar problems, alcohol and sugar cravings.

Venus remediations for physical health and well-being: Eating molecularly whole sugars (such as fruits, dates, maple syrup, molasses, or raw honey), balancing the blood sugar (through a sustained diet high in good fats, protein, vegetables, and complex carbohydrates), reading books such as *The Low Blood Sugar Solution* or *Blood Sugar for Dummies*.

Venus remediations for emotional health and well-being: Socializing, listening to music, going out to fancy restaurants, beautifying the self with clothing and make-up, doting on the self and others, wearing fancy jewelry and other accessories, connecting with people on all levels, finding commonality in all situations, wearing pleasant scents and unguents, smiling and laughing, having a fun outlet that does not honor rule-making. Arranging flowers, giving compliments, words of affirmation, giving and receiving gifts, eating any food that is made with creativity and love, dancing, listening to music, reading fancy food magazines, getting a spa treatment, taking in the arts.

♀

Because Venus is a benefic planet and generally brings experiences that are positive, remediations for Venus are often not necessary. There are instances where the natal Venus is maltreated. This can often show up in health problems that relate to the balance of glucose in the cells, such as diabetes or hypoglycemia. Cell glucose is directly related to our ability to perceive and emit beauty rays.

One example of a hard configuration, is a connection between Venus and Uranus. A Venus/Uranus contact can allow a person to to reinvent the self through creativity, love and communing in general. Because of the electrified and unpredictable nature of the blood sugar balance in this chart, a Venus/Uranus person can often experience unexpected changes in the way they perceive the object of their affections. A Venus/Uranus person will best be suited to an exciting partnership that allows for some electricity in the realm of affection. A sugar-balancing remediation might be used for a

Venus/Uranus aspect if the person has decided that they want to settle down, have children, etc. The need for enlivening through love and the arts should also be given an outlet other than sudden, unexpected break-ups and new mergings. The sign and house of the natal Venus must also be considered when finding appropriate activities.

A Venus/Saturn contact will require an entirely different approach. Venus and Saturn can create feelings of coldness and separation in love and a lack of the beauty needs being met or expressed. A Saturn/Venus conjunction will need to be warmed up if there is a desire in the chart for love and beauty to be expressed. The intent of Saturn is to separate and show distinction, while Venus likes to commune and connect. The two planets can often work in opposition to one another. This is the exact reason why a trine between Venus and Saturn does not feel good to most people. With this combination, it can be quite useful to create new systems of beauty or to understand beauty as a distinct and individualized trait, encompassing many different factors. Playing old time, traditional, or classical music, can help to alleviate the suffering. Structural art projects, needlepoint, knitting, and sewing are also good uses of this configuration. These activities give the Venus/Saturn individual an opportunity to create their own three-dimensional representations of beauty and creativity.

Venus and Pluto together are fixative in nature. The best use of this intense need to connect and transform is through the arts. The nature of the art and transformation will depend on the signs and houses of the planets. It is extremely important to give a Venus/Pluto person an outlet to create and transform. For example, if the Venus/Pluto contact is a conjunction in Virgo, the person might run into problems, aesthetically critiquing the self and lovers, attempting to constantly transform the details of beauty. A Venus/Pluto in Virgo can in fact create artwork that it is extremely profound in its crispness, with an interesting use of color, lighting and detail. In love relationships, however, an artist such as this might also notice tiny details such as physical imperfections and fashion problems.

A Venus/Jupiter square could cause problems, inasmuch as it is overly optimistic in its affections. A chart such as this will need a myriad of social and creative outlets to be put to use on transits to the Venus/Jupiter. If a Venus/Jupiter person wants to have better boundaries, then it will be even more important to have outlets for these exuberant vibrations. Such opportunities could be facilitated through creative projects with other people, outings to concerts, or art shows.

11.5 Mars

Mars vibrations: Heating, aggravating, poking, contentious, energizing, inciting, pushing, impassioning, active, and prodding.

Mars needs: The need to be passionate, instigate, roughhouse, sweat, rage, contend, move fast, and express the internal animal instincts.

People who represent Mars: Ultimate fighters, rock climbers, body builders, pioneers, trailblazers, hikers, instigators, athletes, debaters, warriors, contenders.

Problematic presentations of Mars: Anger, rage, fevers, not wanting to sit still, wanting to pop out of one's body, the urge to explode, wanting to hurt the self or others, sexual frustration.

Mars remediations for physical health and well-being: Acupuncture, rolfing, icing an inflammation or injury, tea tree oil, iodine, antibiotics for infections, hydrotherapy (see below), creams for certain rashy problems, exercise and sports of all kinds, balancing the adrenals through diet and exercise.

Mars remediations for emotional health and well-being: Sports, working out, weightlifting, tattooing, piercing, house projects, consensual sadomasochism, airing one's grievances, running, jogging, venting, being passionate, being feisty, general roughhousing, skateboarding, mountain biking, yelling, wrestling, demolition, gardening, pushing through problems, contending, head banging, adventures and shenanigans, text-fighting, sex, board games, taking off a layer of clothing, watching ultimate fighting or wrestling.

Many Mars illnesses can be mitigated by alternating between hot and cold temperatures. This process seems to expel excess heat and help a person relax. What we are seeking in a Mars remediation is cortisol release. In naturopathic medicine, the process of hydrotherapy can be used to work out a fever. Adults often clean toxins and clear heat build-up through the use of hot tubs, sweat lodges, or hot springs. This experience can also be had by alternating between a hot sauna and a cold lake. One way to alternate between hot and cold with children, is to turn the shower on, steam up the bathroom, wrap a hot towel (covered by a dry towel) around the child's chest, then after five minutes, replace the hot towel with a cold towel. Alternate until the child is sleepy and spent.

Mars is a tricky planet to remediate due to it's hot, rambunctious, and sharp nature. Mars incites our personal will and must be expressed. The suppression of Mars energies can be extremely detrimental to both physical and emotional health. Mars most likely affects both testosterone and cortisol release, and could be said to trigger our "fight or flight" response. The sign and placement of Mars will indicate the areas of life into which we draw martian energies, and how we can most purposefully express our divine will.

Athletics are a perfect release for martian energy. Sporty activities incite passion within people. Exercise of all kinds is beneficial to our emotional and physical happiness. A look at the chart will indicate the athletic activities that will best match the needs of an individual. The simple art of walking can be just the kind of balancing exercise we need. Group athletics are more appropriate if there is a strong eleventh house focus or a strong aquarian tendency. If Mars is in Taurus, heavy lifting might be a good choice, as the energy is slower and more apt towards building and pushing. A Pisces rising might enjoy swimming. One-on-one athletics are better suited for Mars in Libra. If Mars is in Leo, there must be an element of fun and adventure to the athletic experience. Mars in Virgo might enjoy gymnastics for its precise and particular nature. Mars needs an outlet. It needs to contend. Athletics are the perfect activity for such energies.

Certain charts do in fact indicate a suppression of Mars. With Mars/Saturn aspects we often see chronic inflammation. This can present as rheumatism, eczema, rashes, asthma, or arthritis. These problems can and will present in the parts of the body indicated by the signs activated in the aspect. When there does exist a natal aspect from Saturn to Mars, Mars must still be expressed. Without an outlet for this energy, malady will almost certainly present in the physical body. These individuals might be better suited to long walks and other less vigorous types of activity. The Saturn influence might also be mitigated through sports in which there exists a benchmark system, such as throwing a shot-put or discus, or pole-vaulting. In these sports, the athlete is continually trying to improve upon their own score. Another example of working with Saturn would be the engagement in a sport which requires focus and containment, such as tightrope walking, being a pitcher or catcher, or even synchronized swimming.

If the chart is found to have a Mars/Jupiter connection, then the problematic possibilities of Mars will be quite different. A Mars/Jupiter connection can indicate an over-exuberance of martian energies, which can produce some interesting behaviors. The person might be accident prone, physically and sexually, as the need to express one's drive is quite high in this case. These are the types of athletes to want to run marathons, as they are buoyant and optimistic while moving their physical bodies. These types also like to go hiking, have adventures, and engage in other kinds of activities that require a great deal of energy and excitement. These are the triathletes. If Mars and Jupiter are overactive in the life and are causing problems, then they must be provided with a high-energy outlet and a balancing diet.

A Mars/Venus connection will bring a love of the social aspect of sports. This is a good aspect for team sports, or possibly sports requiring a partner and a bit of creativity, such as pairs figure skating, rock climbing, doubles tennis, etc. Mars/Uranus aspects will need a sport that includes an element of excitement and surprise. Mountain biking, scavenger hunting, and skateboarding are great Mars/Uranus activities. Hockey might also work, since one never knows when he or she will be checked into the boards. Mars/Neptune aspects can create the need for a physical expression of softness and illusion. This could manifest through dance, illusion-based theater, swimming, hot yoga, trapeze artistry, or pilates. Mars/Pluto aspects require sports that are intense. Rugby, grappling, martial arts, karate, or ultimate fighting are examples.

11.6 Jupiter

Jupiter vibrations: Opening, joy-filling, growing, uplifting, faith-bringing, optimistic, billowing, lightening, expansive, buoyant, energizing.

Jupiter needs: The need to feel lucky and glorious, be open, grow, be optimistic, take chances, not worry, feel like everything is going to be alright, go with the flow, be jolly, and feel limitless.

People who represent Jupiter: Ministers, travelers, teachers, exchange students, gamblers, comedians, mascots for sports teams, olympic athletes (with Mars prominent), international journalists, philosophers, keynote lecturers, motivational speakers.

Problematic presentations of Jupiter: Being overly optimistic, making plans that cannot be kept, over-spending, inviting too many people over for a party, over-estimating how many resources are available, over-opportunism, not being able to focus, problems with the liver, fatty accumulations, lack of joy.

Jupiter remediations for physical health and well-being: Going on adventures, jovial and spiritual dancing, providing outlets for the freedom-needing energies, liver cleansing, eating only good fats, ingesting fat-soluble vitamins of all kinds, balancing sugar intake so the liver doesn't have to work so hard, eating meats from grass-fed animals who have lived a joyful life, ingesting omega-3 fatty acids, flax oil, or fish oil.

Jupiter remediations for emotional health and well-being: Meeting new people, taking hold of opportunities, creating opportunities, giving to others, being grandiose, laughing and bringing good cheer, traveling, enjoying optimistic philosophies. Learning new concepts that open up the mind to joy, praying and manifesting, laughing contagiously, telling jokes and watching comedians, learning about new ways to feel light and free within the physical form, giving the body the experience of weightlessness, eating immaculately every day, flying to new lands, riding a train to an unknown destination, singing soul music or religious music, remembering the immortal and lifeless soul through some avenue of life.

♃

It seems antithetical in some ways to discuss remediation in relation to the benefic planets. In my opinion, there is no need to even think about remediating Jupiter unless it is causing problems repeatedly, such as in the case of severe obesity (that the client wants to change), growths, or the inability to reign in the desires in some area of life. Jupiter, in the most simplest of descriptions, could called "the expander." Jupiter allows us the optimistic feelings to open ourselves up. Jupiter also brings the feeling of buoyancy, the feeling that everything will be okay, and the need to reach out and become more awesome in some form or fashion. Jupiter reminds us to to have fun and feel joyful, which often accompanies a lack of attention to the constraints of the physical realm.

When remediating an overactive Jupiter we must provide a buoyant and joyful outlet. It will not work to restrain an unrestrained Jupiter. Just as Mars needs an outlet, Jupiter needs to be able to express its billowing and expansive feelings. In other words, it does not work to tell a Jupiterian person to stop being so happy and joyful. This is like telling Santa Claus to stop giving presents to children. Jupiter is meant to be joyful and expansive!

Like any other planet, Jupiter can get out of balance. Saturnian remediations such as dietary management, setting boundaries in relationships, or consulting a teacher or authority figure for guidance can help to control overly-expansive jupiterian energies.

11.7 Saturn

Saturn vibrations: Tightening, constricting, dense, heavy, cold, pressurizing, stressing, structuring, focused, constructive, solidifying, limiting, congealing.

Saturn needs: The need to feel the limitations of incarnation, survive within institutions and shared realities, evolve and improve, create boundaries, create structure, have internal feelings of separation from others, feel constriction, experience stress, and manifest a better life.

People who represent Saturn: Doctors, upstanding citizens, managers, scientists, builders, organizers, mayors, politicians, parents, grandparents, principals, managers, experts, rule-makers, board members, chair persons.

Problematic presentations of Saturn: Blockages, problems with authority figures, feeling stifled, feeling labeled, being unable to express oneself, writer's block, being too cold, emotionally unavailable, experiencing chronic pain or physical constriction, necrosis of tissue, feeling critical of one's work. Feeling sorry for oneself, adhering to all the rules out of fear, quitting tasks that are difficult, complaining, blaming people, taking medication for depression, shaming ourselves and others.

Saturn remediations for physical health and well-being: Deep massage, dental work, chiropractic care, going to an orthopedist, drinking teas with high levels of calcium and magnesium (such as oat-straw or nettles), drinking broths and miso, pressing on the body, squeezing pressurized areas, structural care (broken bone repair, casts, splints), grooming and cleaning the skin, detoxing the organs, regimented physical exercise that is not overly heating (walking, stretching, or yoga), seeing an expert or specialist, physical therapy in water (Saturn can stiffen the body), warming methods of healing, such as moxibustion.

Saturn remediations for emotional health and well-being: Working, time alone to continue working, practicing, discipline, scheduling things, self-imposed rules, boundaries, silence (when in combination with Mercury), distance, contrived separation, creating circumstances that incite longing, self-imposed deadlines, persistent effort, being squeezed or held tight, clearing clutter, building a structure or manifesting a new creation, profound and deep study, physical labor, writing up a contract, making a budget, practicing rudiments, introspection, the use of old or antique items, engaging in classical experiences, assigning a duty or role to oneself, being tied up or constrained, being bound or corseted, acting as a mentor, organizing something, being regimented, asking a dominatrix to make the rules for you, working towards being an expert in some area, setting goals for oneself.

♄

It is quite difficult to feel free and lighthearted when under the influence of Saturn. Saturn is not a planet that incites feelings of freedom and joy. Saturn clearly siphons into us an experience of being schooled or constrained in some area of the life. Saturn triggers stress and pressure, while at the same time constricting certain bodily functions, such as enzymatic reactions, glycolysis, thermal-cellular reactions, the formation of tissue, etc. Because of its constrictive emissions, Saturn incites fear, inadequacies, loneliness, depression, and an internal experience of feeling cut off from others. It is important to over-nourish the body under extreme, saturnian conditions, as this can compensate for a lack of mineral absorption, or any other suppressed body functions. The constriction will most likely be in the area of the body ruled by the sign in which Saturn is placed.

At any age, we can feel stressed under the weight of authority figures. Children tend to differentiate themselves from parents and teachers under the influence of Saturn, as they begin to feel confined by rules and structures. In the teenage years, both parental rules and societal expectations give language to our internal feelings of separation. A senior citizen might experience Saturn through their entire physical being, as health constrictions become more prevalent in old age. In fact, Saturn could be said to constantly remind us that we are in a congealed, three-dimensional, human form and that we are limited on account of this structure. Our bodies need to eat. We need to put food on the table. We need to not break our bones. These are the lessons that Saturn teaches us.

When a child has a very strong natal Saturn, it is very important to begin remediation from a young age. These children can be quite susceptible to overly high self-expectations. This quality can also create exceptionally good public behavior. It will be important to allow these children to experience the more natural side of Saturn's consequences, inasmuch as they may naturally feel fearful and inadequate. In fact, these kids need very little encouragement in order to actually live up to expectations, as these same personality traits create a drive to work hard and excel. It can be beneficial to encourage a child with high self-expectations to create his or her own important role. Certain kids will find solace in picking an activity which they want to practice, as this will allow them a healthy outlet through which to strive and improve.

If there exists a tight aspect to Saturn in the chart of an adult, there will exist a feeling of being burdened by the constraints of life. The places in which we feel separate, different, or inadequate will depend upon the houses, signs, and planetary aspects involved. Susceptibility to Saturn's constriction varies. Many charts do not have an intense, natal Saturn configuration. Everyone has at times experienced the weight of Saturn, yet some people are extremely prone to becoming downtrodden by these forces.

On account of the stressful nature of Saturn, it is important to remediate carefully. The remediations for the vibrations of Saturn are not always glorious nor fun. The real-life emotional and physical experience of transits to and from Saturn can be painful and frustrating. There can exist the misconception that once a person knows when the energies will be coming in and out of their life through the use of astrology, they will then float happily through the influences of Saturn. This is far from the truth. Saturn calls for us to remember plainly and clearly that we have incarnated into the three-dimensional plane. The exact manner in which each of us feels this separation depends entirely on the precise position of Saturn in the natal chart or by transit.

For example, we are taught that in good relationships we are to feel connected and warm with our partners, forever being happy to see them and wanting to touch their bodies. Saturn can bring up feelings of internal separation. Suppose that a person were to have Venus sitting in their house of partnership. If Saturn were to travel up to the position of Venus and stop there for three months, the bearer of the chart would be forced to remember the inherent separation between himself and his partner, even though the normal state of Venus in this place is to love and be sweet.

The influence of Saturn can often create heavy situations, for which there is no easy way out. While remediations may not entirely erase the negative feelings associated with Saturn, the feelings of frustration, shame, and anguish can in fact be lessened.

11.8 Uranus

Uranus vibrations: Electric, inciting, jumpy, high-vibrating, chaotic, penetrating, exciting, innovating, revolutionizing, changing, moving, explosive, and frenetic.

Uranus needs: The need to evolve quickly, revolt, be excited, be transformed, change one's situation, be electric, be amped up, experience the unexpected, not have patience, and be interesting.

People who represent Uranus: Antagonizers, protesters, rebels, pioneers, inventors, quantum physicists, electricians.

Problematic presentations of Uranus: Excessive use of stimulants, hasty decision-making, compulsive use of social media or other modern technologies, erratic behavior, seizures.

Uranus remediations for physical health and well-being: Abstaining from stimulants, allowing the body to twitch and move, dancing to electronic music, trying new and daring physical activities.

Uranus remediations for emotional health and well-being: Going with the flow, allowing the self to evolve, being emotionally inventive, doing things your own way, being revolutionary, doing things that enliven and lighten the self, being rebellious.

Uranus is a tricky planet, inasmuch as it seems to go against the crystallizing nature of Saturn. Uranus forces us to get out of ruts, revolutionize ourselves, and emerge on new paths. Uranus can feel as if we drank a bunch of coffee, took uppers, or are just really excited. Uranus is also linked to seizures, spasms, and anxiety.

The best way to remediate Uranus is to accept that unexpected changes are a part of life. I have witnessed many plans change during Uranus transits. Perhaps Uranus is the planet that allows even astrologers and psychics to be surprised. From Uranus, we learn important lessons of anti-crystallization, collapse, and regeneration. That is what Uranus is meant to do. It keeps life interesting.

Highly uranian individuals seek experiences that are enlivening, such as taking stimulant drugs, drinking a lot of coffee, and bungee jumping. They might also be involved in creating new ways of living and revolutionizing life. One of the best remediations for such an energy is to sit back and enjoy the ride. It is futile to try to get a person to settle down in the area of life that is being revolutionized by Uranus. In certain charts that are excessively saturnian, it will also be important to help the client consider ways in which to find variety within structures, such as working a stable freelance job or three steady part-time jobs.

If Uranus were in contact with Venus, perhaps the remediation could be a non-monogamous relationship. This is not the only option, as the uranian vibration could also be honored through a relationship that is rich with role playing, or is extreme or non-conventional in some other way. Perhaps having a partner who is a body modification expert, world traveler, or nuclear physicist would suffice.

If Uranus is producing problems in relation to Mercury, the remediation must be mental. There must be a cerebral outlet for the excitement, such as fast-paced communications, challenging interactions, etc.

Suppose Uranus were to hit Pluto by transit; the revolution would be deep and transformative. In this case, deep psychotherapy might be helpful; the type to tear down and revolutionize the soul and energy-body.

The general principles to remember when working with Uranus are innovation, change, and excitement. Invention can be prescribed, as can activities that are entirely new to the person, but are not stressful nor compressive. Think verve, electricity, and rejuvenation.

11.9 Neptune

Neptune vibrations: Diffuse, softening, gaseous, amorphous, magical, floating, dreamy, sleep-inducing, psychic, confusing, spiritual, soft, illusional.

Neptune needs: The need to sleep and snuggle, channel art and music, merge with others, experience magic and miracles, feel inspired, seek divinity, seek transcendence, attend to the psychic and spiritual self, and respond to vibrations.

People who represent Neptune: Psychics, idealists, performers, thespians, martial artists, magicians, illusionists, hallucinators, sleepwalkers, people who have night terrors, nappers, narcoleptics, reiki masters, preachers, spiritual teachers.

Problematic presentations of Neptune: Lies, confusion, dementia, alcoholism, allergies, sleepiness, illnesses of an undiagnosable variety, syndromes, lack of resolution or the option for it, the feeling of being energetically compromised, feeling fatigued, psychic struggles, extreme sensitivity, the frequent urge to weep, endocrine imbalances, sensitivity to light and sound.

Neptune remediations for emotional health and well-being: Homeopathic remedies, swimming, sleep, attaching a higher meaning to events in the life, meditation, reiki, snuggling, gems, aromatherapy, music, photography, painting, shamanic journeys, sitting in a mineral bath, angel readings, surrounding the self with good vibrations, learning the language of astrology, crying.

Neptune remediations for physical health and well-being: Apple cider vinegar (for changing Ph balance in fungal problems), tea tree oil, fermented foods (for candida problems, food allergies, and abnormal cell growth), exorcisms, the use of a medical intuitive, systemic treatments (such as high level doses of vitamin C for cancer), sitting in hot springs or mineral baths, fluid-releasing activities (such as lymph drainage and ejaculation), clearing the energy field with certain vibrational instruments (such as tuning forks, a well-played didgeridoo, or an electromagnetic machine of some variety).

It is very hard to be neptunian in our modern society, as the structures can be rigid and unaccepting of perceptive variation. Certain cultures have greatly valued the Neptune experience. We have seen this in many native cultures, where two-spirited people, shamans, and other soul-healers are valued. A neptunian ideal also exists in cultures in which the language is constructed to focus on the vibrational beauty of life and the emotional health of humanity. Neptunian experiences are valued in most places or groups which embrace and cherish perceptive variation and vibrance.

Feelings and emotional undercurrents are extremely important to certain people. The sense of vulnerability created by such strong emotions creates a need for trust. We most often trust people who tell us the truth. For a parent, this might come in the form of a sense or feeling that something is upsetting their child. Perhaps a parent notices that their child seems tired and disconnected recently. The parent might wonder what is causing this new tendency. When asked what the problem is, the child may respond that "nothing is wrong." The parent in this case will most likely not *trust* this response. The words uttered by the child in this case do not match the energy that the child is expressing. By communicating what we feel inside, an experience of shared reality and wholeness between individuals is created.

In their most basic form, Neptune problems debilitate trust. Whether the neptunian difficulty is presenting through alcoholism, hallucinations, dementia, or psychic messages, each situations creates tension inasmuch as there is a lack of a shared reality. There are an infinite number of situations in which a lack of shared reality exists. An alcoholic wife may not remember her actions the next day, while her husband does. A prophetess might get a strong feeling about something, yet lack any confirmation from the world around her. Until the day that the prophecy does become a structural reality, there will be a disconnect in shared reality with the world around her. In the highest sense, Neptune seeks to release us from the reality-constraints of Saturn by denying us the opportunity to share perceptive assimilation.

People who have charts that like structure and authority don't tend to be neptunian individuals. They tend to be more of the saturnian temperament, as these persons hold within them the skills to build and maintain structures for the Neptune people to play upon. When a neptunian person is forced to behave and interpret information in a saturnian manner, it can be quite deflating. For instance, when a prophecy is treated as untrue on account of having not yet manifested, then the person's perceptive reality is treated as deficient.

It is extremely important that we adopt a value structure that allows for Neptune individuals to flourish. Neptune allows us to jump the veil into dreamland. Some people dream while sleeping, and others dream while awake.

When a strong Neptune is present, the act of artistic channeling is an extremely important skill which must be cultivated. It could be said that channeling is the art of manifesting the dreamy world of Neptune into a perceivable structure. A psychic channel will be bringing the impressions they feel to others through spoken words. An artistic channel might construct paper objects or paintings that are borne from their own special experience. A musical channel will play out their internal vibratory experience.

In children, we call neptune experiences "imagination." Kids naturally channel their imagination through art projects, imagination play, and storytelling. As we grow older, we are expected to tone down our imaginative values and get to "work."

Certain individuals have in fact incarnated to maintain earthly structures and shared realities, and these people might not respond much to energetic vibrations. These are the types who have been created to be robust and solid (often working as bricklayers and other foundational artists) and are put on earth to bring the gifts of structure to the world around us. It could also be said that there are people who have been put here to bring vibrational beauty to the earth plane, and these persons are often quite hard for the structure-keepers to understand.

While a structure-keeper will become derailed by a structural fallout, such as a changing educational milieu or the collapse of social security benefits, an energetically sensitive person is more likely to be overwhelmed by bad thoughts coming at them from another person in the room, or a flurry of excitement or anger. In these moments, energetic waves of emotion are sent out into the vibrational atmosphere and fall upon the sensorily sensitive person, causing a flare up of the astral body.

Certain people can in fact excel in highly specialized areas because their receptors are attuned to certain stimuli. Their bodies seem to naturally understand a language of energy that other people's do not. Challenges with vibrationally special children often occur on account of perception variations. Kids who get diagnosed with behavioral problems do so because they are somehow disruptive within the institutions that currently exist. It could be most simply said that most institutions find perceptive variation and shared reality to be mutually exclusive.

A prominent Neptune can allow people to channel information from the upper realms. This can come in the form of music, words, concepts, art, visual images, or anything that seems to be overly surreal and not helping out all that much with the structural needs of life. When this tendency is affecting a person's life in a detrimental manner, mental health institutions try to manage these variations in perception through diagnostic tools and the grouping of symptoms. This kind of Neptune management occurs in schools, hospitals, psychology offices, and more.

One of the challenges of receiving psychic messages is that they don't seem to have any adherence to earthly institutions such as clock-time. Neptune intends to take us to the divine place. This also happens to be the place that doesn't value the harsh existence of material and earthly reality. In a good aspect, Neptune can remind us to relax and harken the messages of idealism that exist around us. In a hard aspect, Neptune can make us feel far too sensitive to deal with keeping up with the institution-driven "rat race."

When treating a medical problem involving a very strong natal Neptune, it will be very important to use finesse. If the remedial is too harsh, the Neptune problem will most likely get worse. The reason for this is that the problem is often not of a physical nature, and should be treated on more of a vibrational and soul-needs basis.

Common Neptune Problems

1. Difficulties, confusion, and skewed perception of reality within interpersonal relations.

2. Others benefiting from the neptunian energy more than the individual. This can be remedied by teaching the Neptune person how to protect their energy-field and avoid codependent relationships.

3. People negating the reality of the person who is having the Neptune experience.

4. Neptune can create people who are fascinating and inspirational, yet sensitive and highly attuned to a variety of otherworldly experiences.

5. Neptunian individuals can emit an energy that makes it hard for others to take them seriously.

6. Neptune can create people who are extremely loving and understanding of the human struggle, and may feel an overwhelming sense of guilt and responsibility to "heal the world" at the expense of their own well-being.

11.10   Pluto

Pluto vibrations: Penetrating, focused, pressurized, digging, fixating, dark, morbid, relentlessly deep, thick, soul-bonding, power-filling, and otherworldly.

Pluto needs: The need to die and be reborn, take it to the limit, attach the soul to something, be transformed entirely, transmute, become unrecognizable to oneself, go deep, and be drastically and forever changed.

People who represent Pluto: Excavators, morticians, recyclers, re-builders, depth psychologists, hypnotherapists, shamans, intense people, qi-gong masters, plutonian physicists, composting specialists, sewer cleaners, colonic irrigation specialists.

Problematic presentations of Pluto: Fixation, cheating, obsessive love, obsessive addictions, being agitated on a level of the inner consciousness, power struggles, intensity, stalking, abusive relationships.

Pluto remediations for emotional health and well-being: Depth psychology, art projects of great magnitude or scale, flying or other death-defying activities, driving a race car, body modification, purification rituals, scarification, group therapy, melting metal or welding, confronting death, going to a cemetery, being guided through a soul retrieval ceremony, getting a cord-clearing, unleashing nuclear-like power through a musical instrument, changing one's identity.

Pluto remediations for physical health and well-being: Surgery, radiation, amputation, re-structural healing (such as ongoing chiropractic treatment or intense massage), training for a marathon, swimming the english channel, getting a colonic irrigation, transforming one's DNA, asking the highest of all divine beings for a miracle, intensely altering the lifestyle, tearing down and rebuilding the whole diet (when the Moon is involved).

♇

Due to their extreme nature, plutonian problems can be hard to manage. As a young astrologer, it was very hard for me to figure out how to really help people through these challenges. These transits and natal configurations are very fixative. This obsessive nature could also be associated with traits that are seemingly unstoppable, deep, perpetually focused, and subconsciously fearful. Pluto does not follow logic, but instead creates a death-ray in a certain area in the life. This kind of experience can manifest through anything from having to change one's name or go into hiding, to grieving one's own death.

When someone around us is going through a hard Pluto transit, it can be hard to not get caught up in their intensity, as the energy is truly powerful and deep. Energy-moving activities can be great Pluto remediations! Qi gong, for instance, pulls and moves these intense vibrations around. Playing heavy, dark music would also be a good outlet for the emotions that build up under Pluto's rays. The best use of Pluto is to channel its rays into a deep understanding and use of the sign and house involved, and to take actions which allow for transformation to occur in those areas.

12
The Signs in Remediation

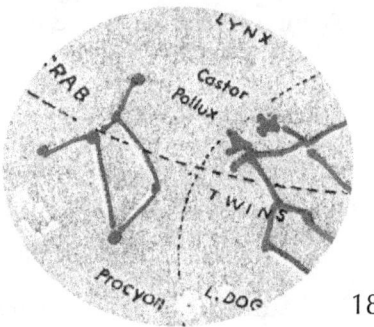

The zodiacal signs are the celestial filters through which the wavelengths, frequencies, & photonic energies of the celestial bodies are expressed and experienced.

---

[18] Image from the book entitled *Find the Constellations*, by H.A. Rey, the same author who wrote the *Curious George* series!

Aries: Trailblazing, hot, adventurous, igniting.

Taurus: Stable, patient, resourcing, fixed, foundational, steady.

Gemini: Changeable, lingual, fast, cerebral, synaptic.

Cancer: Nourishing, nostalgic, protective, nurturing, historical, coveting.

Leo: Proud, fun, joyful, individualized, hearty.

Virgo: Particular, precise, discerning, bodily, practical, servile, detailing.

Libra: Balancing, compromising, diplomatic, charming, connecting, curious.

Scorpio: Intense, penetrating, transforming, mesmerizing, deepening, steaming.

Sagittarius: Joyful, freeing, enthusiastic, quirky, unpredictable, moving.

Capricorn: Industrious, building, tangible, persevering, structuring, hierarchical.

Aquarius: Political, grouping, humanitarian, conventioning, corralling, categorizing.

Pisces: Sensing, ethereal, pictoral, diffuse, magical, inspiring, conceptual.

The signs are very important in remediation and will show the manner in which the planetary needs will emerge. The key to astrological remediation is to understand the urges of the planet, to combine this with a person's natural way of expressing the energy of that planet. In medical astrology, the signs are connected to the parts of the body in which a malady will show up. This presents an obvious link between the signs and healing. The needs of a planet will be filtered through the sign in which that planet is sitting. As remedialists, we will want to know what the soul is craving, as this will clue us into the kinds of activities or remedies that will most effectively relieve suffering. Any budding remedialist can begin an analysis of a chart by combing the key description words to a planet associated with the sign in which that planet is situated. Let us present an example here, so that we may get acquainted with this process.

If the planet of Venus is in the sign of Leo, then the needs of Venus are combined with the keywords of Leo, so that we might better understand the cravings of the soul.

Venus: The need to commune, connect, bond, be appealing, exchange sweetness and adoration, and emit beauty.

Leo: Proud, fun, joyful, individualized, hearty.

The need to commune in a fun manner. The need to connect in an individualized way. The need to bond in a hearty way. The need to be appealing on account of individuality. The need to give and receive sweetness through fun. The need to be joyfully adored.

The need to glow proudly. The need for proud, fun and hearty eros-love.

Now, let us present two examples that are quite different than Venus in Leo; Saturn in Aquarius and Saturn in Pisces.

Saturn: The need to feel the limitations of incarnation, survive within institutions and shared realities, evolve and improve, create boundaries, create structure, have internal feelings of separation from others, feel constriction, experience stress, and manifest a better life.

Aquarius: Political, grouping, humanitarian, conventioning.

The need to feel the limitations of incarnation through the political sphere. The need to survive within categorized, shared realities. The need to experience institutionalization through groupings. The need for a humanitarian structure. The need for an internal feeling of separation within groups. The need for constriction through the political sphere. The need to experience stress through groupings of people.

And now we combine the needs of Saturn with the qualities of Pisces.

The need to feel the limitations of incarnation through concepts. The need to understand the shared realities of magic. The need to understand conceptual institutions. The need to grow and improve through the ethereal realm. The need for inspiring structures. The need for an internal feeling of sensory separation. The need to experience sensory stress.

When remediating problems with any planet, we tend to find the most success by working with the natural tendencies of the sign involved. Let us continue to develop a base of knowledge that will aid us in developing our techniques, by delving into the portions of earthly life that will tug at our inner-sphere, otherwise known as *the houses*.

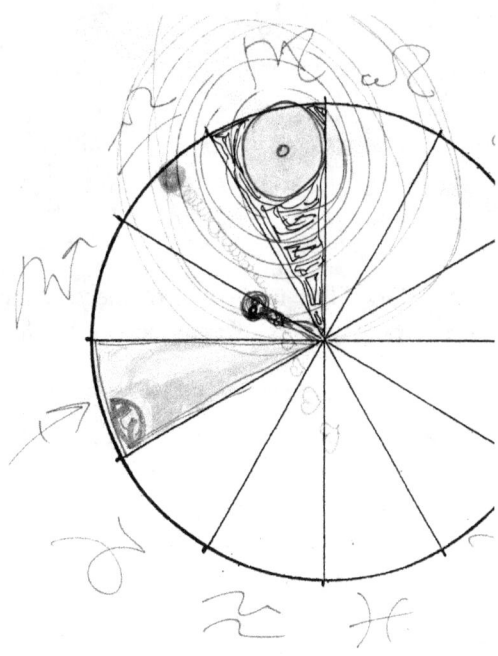

13 The Houses:

Areas of life into which the vibes of the planets can be expressed.

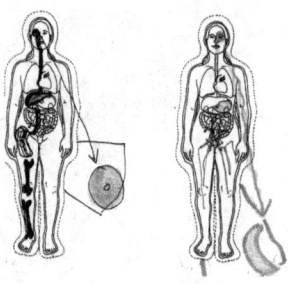

House One: The institution of the self, the role in every sphere, the physical body, the identity, the foundation of the chart.

House Two: Institutions of resource management, money, food, the foundation of exchange.

House Three: The microcosmic social sphere, short trips, siblings, the neighborhood, remedial education, the institutions that facilitate concept-exposure and language formation.

House Four: The nourishing resource foundation, the nurturing institutions, home, property, land, the past in general.

House Five: Joy, creativity, fun, self-expression, children, amusement, foundations of inspiration.

House Six: The institution of time, daily work, the health habits, the foundation of employment.

House Seven: The institution of partnership, close engagement with others, building through equal exchange, marriage.

House Eight: Institutions of transformation, power, other people's resources, foundations of timelessness.

House Nine: Institutions facilitating new or high-minded concept-formation, long-distance travel, higher education, religion, philosophy, foundations of growth through experience.

House Ten: The institution of reputation, the professional resources, career, engagement with the public.

House Eleven: The institution of groups, community, political and identity clusters, shared hopes and dreams.

House Twelve: The institution of the subconscious, the hidden and repressed realms, the foundation of unspoken realities.

Having examined both the urges of the planets and their need for expressions through each of the signs, we now must begin adding to our analysis the indications of the houses. The houses in astrology represent the areas of life into which we focus our specific energies. The sign will show the manner in which planetary vibes will most easily be expressed into specific areas of life, as indicated by the houses. A thorough analysis of the planets, signs and houses can be performed through a simple process. First, we look to the needs and vibrational nature of the planet. We then combine these qualities with the natural tendencies of the sign.

Next, we look to the keywords and areas of life indicated by the house placement. This process will allow us to identify a number of ways to put language upon what is happening with a certain planet in any given chart. When we have learned how to think about this planetary influence in relation to the needs and intent underneath, we can then begin writing up lists of remediations. The more we think about charts in reference to the soul-needs, the better we will become at moving through this process of analysis. Let's continue to build on the examples used in the previous chapter.

Saturn in Aquarius in houses 4, 5, & 12.

Formula: Planetary urges, vibrations, and needs +

Astrological sign + House placement

Saturn in Aquarius:

The need to feel the limitations of incarnation through the political sphere. The need to survive within categorized, shared realities. The need for a humanitarian structure. The need for an internal feeling of separation within groups. The need for constriction through the political sphere. The need to experience stress through groupings of people.

Saturn + Aquarius + Fourth House

House Four: The nourishing resource foundation, the nourishing institutions, home, property, land, the past in general.

The soul will need to feel limitations through the political sphere and within institutions that facilitate and manage emotional resource building. The soul will need to experience social constriction through the sphere of home and family. The soul will crave to build a humanitarian structure through the act of owning property or land.

Saturn + Aquarius + Fifth House

House Five: Joy, creativity, fun, self-expression, children, amusement, foundations of inspiration.

The soul will need to feel limitations through the political sphere and within institutions that facilitate joy and self-expression. The soul will need to experience social constriction through the sphere of amusement, children, and creativity. The soul will crave to build a humanitarian structure through places that value self-expression and creativity.

Saturn + Aquarius + Twelfth House

House Twelve: The institution of the subconscious, the hidden and repressed realms, the foundation of unspoken realities.

The soul will need to feel limitations through the political sphere and within institutions that represent the hidden and repressed realms. The soul will crave to build a humanitarian structure through places that value the institution of the subconscious.

We now understand how to combine, identify, and remediate the urges and vibrations of the planets, in reference to the soul-needs. In the next section, we will learn how to combine the needs of more than one planet, and understand the cyclical behavior of planetary aspects. The astrological aspects could be said to create certain "aspects" of our personality, in that they create clusters of soul-needs that are unique to each of our lives. It is the astrological aspects that make life interesting! As astrologers, an understanding of aspect-clusters is crucial when beginning to watch charts in real time, and also in relation to the past and future. The natal aspects show our lifetime tendencies, while the transiting aspects indicate passing phases in our life. Let us now go deeper into the wonderful world of astrological aspects.

14

The Aspects in Remediation

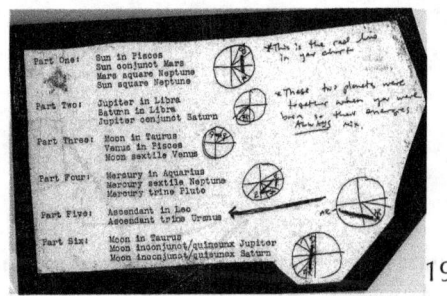

19

Natal aspects are the angular relationships between planets in the natal chart.

Planets in angular relationships to one another indicate clusters of vibrational experience.

The aspects can be imagined as the keyholes in our astral receiver.

---

[19] This is an example of what might be inside a *Secret Envelope*. In this case, the envelope recipient was learning about her *aspect clusters*.

Aspects are the angular configurations between the planets in an astral schematic. In my experience, the aspects in a person's chart are far more descriptive of the lifetime tendencies than the zodiacal signs alone. The signs do in fact describe how the mixing energies of the aspects are expressed stylistically.

A basic example of the astronomy of an aspect is in order.

Suppose a person is born on a day when the Moon is exactly "cut in half" in the night sky. This will mean that the Sun and Moon are 7 days from their last conjunction at the Newmoon (there are approximately 29 days in one Sun/Moon cycle). The Moon moves 13 degrees of a zodiacal sign each day.

$$13 \text{ degrees} \times 7 \text{ days} = 91 \text{ degrees}$$

When the Moon is exactly cut in half in the sky, we know that the Sun and Moon are also 90 degrees apart in zodiacal longitude. Astrologers would then call this 90 degree aspect between the Sun and the Moon a *square* aspect.

Aspects are important because they indicate clusters of energy! The chart at birth will show angles between the planets, and these angles will show how the vibrations mix in the astral receiver. The moving energies of the wandering planets also make angles to parts of the natal chart. A transit to the natal chart brings an energetic influxing to the psyche, which inherently alters the pre-existing urges, needs, and experience of the life.

Oftentimes, a serious behavioral or emotional problem will be shown clearly in the aspect structure of the astrological chart. Hard aspects can create vibrations that are hard to handle. Think of a chord on the piano that is harsh, discordant, or just too loud. In the personality, an intensely hot mixing of planets will create hyper-inspired ways of being, while cold and constrictive combinations tend to create oppression and immobility.

The exact expression of each aspect depends upon the soul inhabiting the chart, as well as the signs and houses in which the planets are sitting. First, let's go ahead with a description of the configurations that we will be using for analysis in the remainder of this book. Listed next are the specific names that astrologers use for each of the angular relationships possible between the planets, stars, etc.

Conventional Aspects [20]

Conjunction: Planets sitting on top of one another. 0 degrees apart.

Semi-sextile: Planets sitting 30 degrees apart. Adjacent signs.

Sextile: Planets sitting 60 degrees and three signs apart.

Square: Planets sitting 90 degrees and four signs apart.

Trine: Planets sitting 120 degrees and five signs apart.

Inconjunct: Planets sitting 150 degrees and six signs apart.

Opposition: Planets sitting 180 degrees and seven signs apart.

Aspects indicate vibrations that will mix within the energy field of the astral receiver, and thus within the auric field and life of a person. Aspects provide access to certain life experiences, as they tie together certain vibrational qualities, signs, and areas of life. It is very important to understand aspects, as these are the basic fundamental building blocks that tie together the vibrations of the entire chart.

---

[20] = a shout out to aspects.

Aspects exist in both western and eastern astrology, and surely soften the *precession of the equinoxes argument* against astrology.

Have I mentioned that aspect-clusters can be examined in *real time*?!?

The process is quite simple and if we do this as a practice, we don't have to *guess* at how certain planets are functioning in any chart.

As remedialists, we will want to understand the concept of astrological *orb*. When astrologers use the term "orb," they are referring to the exactitude of the angle between two planets. For instance, a conjunction with an orb of 1 degree means that two planets are one degree apart. A sextile aspect with an orb of 2 degrees could mean that the two planets are either 58 or 62 degrees from one another. In this book, we will not want to simplify our synthesis of aspects to a simple concept of orb, but will instead want to focus our gaze upon the exact patterning of aspects. The information we will want to know could be covered by questions such as these:

Which planet is activated first by each passing transit?

Is the square a simple 90 degree configuration, or does it also involve another aspect?

How many planets are involved in the aspect cluster?

Is the chart made up of 5 conjunctions or a T-square[21]? If so, what does this mean for the life experience?

Here is an explanation of how to use the aspects when attempting to remediate a problem in the natal chart. When assisting with a tension between two planets, we must provide an outlet for the vibrations of both planets involved. Otherwise, the totality of vibrations will not get expressed, filtered, or balanced through the remediation, and the tension will continue to exist between the two or more areas of the life.

---

[21] T-square = 2 squares and an opposition.

An aspect with four planets will most likely require a list of combined remediations for each of the four planets. If the experience is quite intense, we will want to attend to each of these planets on a physical, emotional, and mental level. As we move through the finer points of the aspects, we will want to understand the manner in which each aspect configuration behaves vibrationally and in connection to cyclical timing. By obtaining this information, we will be empowered to heal and soothe past, present, and future experiences!

Conjunction = 0 degrees

Example: Sun 5 Virgo + Mars 5 Virgo

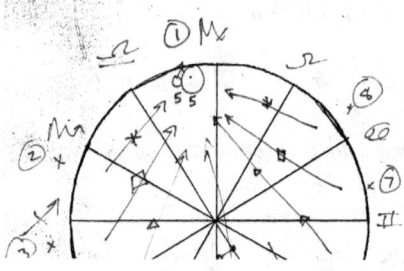

A conjunction could be said to be the aspect that is most pure in form. Any time a transiting planet hits one planet in a conjunction, it always hits the other planet as well. The two planets that mix in a basic conjunction can at times be quite sympathetic to one another. At other times, a conjunction can create challenging and intense experiences.

Mathematically, if we look at one cycle through the zodiacal signs, supposing that the cycle is starting upon the natal conjunction, we notice that this conjunction will be triggered or highlighted through the energies of the transiting planets at the following positions.

1. **0 degrees**   5 Virgo
2. **60 degrees**   5 Scorpio
3. **90 degrees**   5 Sagittarius
4. **120 degrees**   5 Capricorn
5. **180 degrees**   5 Pisces
6. **240 degrees**   5 Taurus
7. **270 degrees**   5 Gemini
8. **300 degrees**   5 Cancer

If we look at the cycles of transits to a conjunction, we will notice that there are 8 major aspects made, beginning with the conjunction itself. It makes sense that, in the case of a conjunction, the planets involved will experience both easy and hard vibrations. A conjunction will at times be hit by a transiting sextile, which is an easy energy. At other times by a square, which can be much more stressful. The nature of a conjunction also depends a great deal on the two planets involved. Certain vibrations mix well together and others are more challenging to manage.

Remedial Considerations: In a conjunction, both planets always mix, and must be considered together. For a problematic conjunction, it will be important to provide remedials on many levels. The transiting influences to the conjunction should also be considered in the nature of the remedies, as the transits will affect the inherent nature of the natal mixing.

Opposition = 180 degrees

Example: Sun 5 Virgo + Mars 5 Pisces

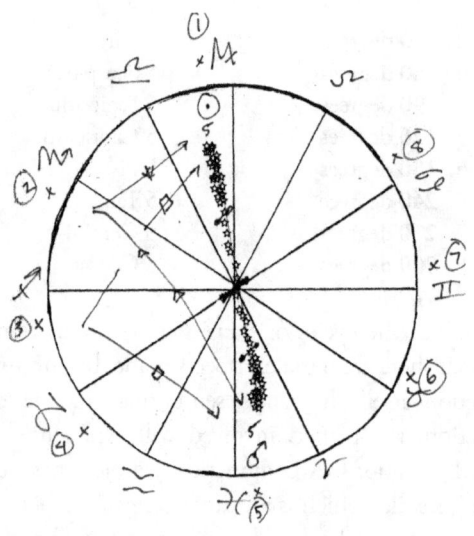

1. **0 degrees**   5 Virgo
2. **60 degrees**   5 Scorpio
3. **90 degrees**   5 Sagittarius
4. **120 degrees**   5 Capricorn
5. **180 degrees**   5 Pisces
6. **240 degrees**   5 Taurus
7. **270 degrees**   5 Gemini
8. **300 degrees**   5 Cancer

Just as with the conjunction, we can see that the opposition is activated eight times throughout the cycle of any planetary orbit, and thus the opposition is an active aspect. Because the 180 degree angle is stressful, needing to simultaneously express into two seemingly opposing areas of life, it behaves a bit like the conjunction, but in a different fashion. With both the conjunction and the opposition, the two energies of the planets always mix. We know this because each time a traveling planet hits one of the planets, it also hits the other. The two planets involved are interacting consistently. An individual with either a conjunction or opposition will have the experience of being privy to a constant mixing of the two vibrations, as neither energy is experienced alone. The conjunction will feel more focused in one area of life, while the opposition feels the needs of two planets at odds.

Remedial Considerations: In an opposition, both planets always mix, and must be considered together. There will be tension at times, as the energies are being channeled in two seemingly opposite spheres of life simultaneously. The signs in an opposition will be of the same mode, but will be of different yet compatible elements. These variations should be considered when providing remedies. For a problematic opposition, it will be important to provide remedials on many levels. The transiting influences to the opposition should also be considered in the nature of the remedies, as the transits will affect the inherent nature of the natal mixing.

Sextile = 60 degrees

Example: Sun 5 Virgo + Mars 5 Scorpio

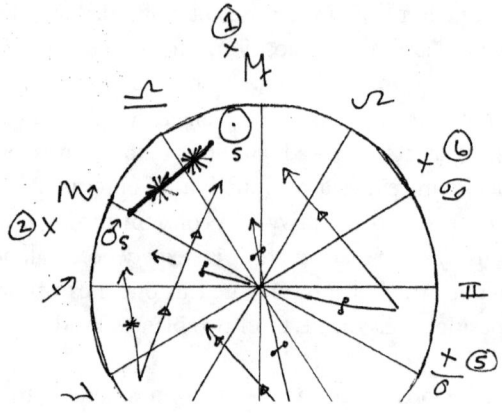

Sextile: Fire/Air, Earth/Water

If we observe one cycle around the chart, we notice that the sextile will be highlighted as follows:

1. 5 Virgo
2. 5 Scorpio
3. 5 Capricorn
4. 5 Pisces
5. 5 Taurus
6. 5 Cancer

The sextile will mathematically be enlivened six times during any one planetary cycle. A sextile will always exist in signs that are in sympathetic elements, providing easy and gracefully-received influxings through the astral receiver. Sextiles can benefit from remediation when they are under the influence of transiting Saturn or Mars. Very often, they are quite easy and pleasant!

Remedial Considerations: The energies will mix six times during a cycle, being expressed and filtered through harmonious elements. Extreme remediations are often not needed. Focus on soft, harmonious remediations when Saturn or Mars are involved.

Trine = 120 degrees

The trine aspect is mathematically similar to the sextile, but is different in that both planets will be of the same element.

Example: Sun 5 Virgo + Mars 5 Capricorn

A traveling planet would ignite this trine at any of these celestial positions:

1. 5 Virgo
2. 5 Scorpio
3. 5 Capricorn
4. 5 Pisces
5. 5 Taurus
6. 5 Cancer

Remedial Considerations: In one planetary cycle, a trine will be highlighted 6 times, and most of these mixings will manifest a healthy and happy experience. A trine is a most fruitful aspect, inasmuch as the two planets in a trine are both in signs of the same element, meaning that they vibrate at the same density of matter. However, each planet in the trine will represent a different rate of matter.

Square = 90 degrees

Example: Sun 5 Virgo + Mars 5 Gemini

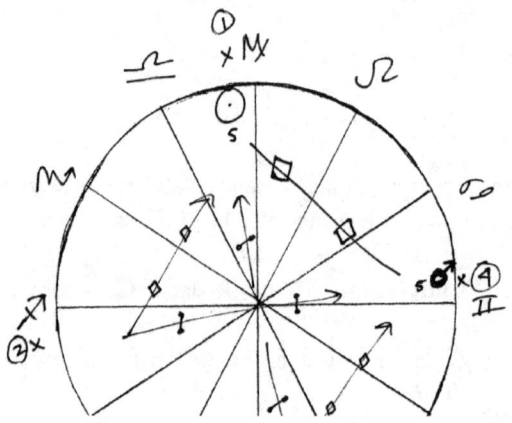

The square aspect is interesting, as it can be an erratic configuration. One concept I have learned from reading the *Anthology* by Vettius Valens is that squares are "anomalous and irregular." The reason for this is actually quite simple. Imagine Jupiter coming up to hit both planets in a square aspect. As Jupiter would form a conjunction with one planet in the square, it would also square the other planet. A billowing and happy-feeling square from Jupiter can be said to be "excessively expansive" or perhaps even "overly glorious." Now imagine Saturn hitting the same square by transit. It will highly compress the abundant energies of the square, which will feel exceedingly different.

In the life of an individual, this means that the vibrations of a square will at times be intensely expansive, and at other times will be exceedingly restrictive. The key to understanding and remediating is to remember that the square does not get highlighted often in the aspect cycle of a planetary orbit. It is more of a sparse yet highly enlivened aspect.

The mixing of the vibrational natures of the signs in a square can at times be a challenge. For example, let us observe the following square:

Sun in Virgo *square* Mars in Gemini

The aspect will become inflamed four times in each cycle, and the seemingly different needs of the Sun in Gemini and Mars in Virgo must be considered simultaneously.

First of all, let us calculate the four positions along the ecliptic:

1. 5 Virgo
2. 5 Sagittarius
3. 5 Pisces
4. 5 Gemini

We notice that each of these points are in mutable signs. In a true 90 degree square aspect, we will always be dealing with signs that vibrate at the same *rate of matter* (astrological modes of cardinal, fixed, and mutable), yet they will always also be of a different *density of matter* (different elements, such as water, fire, air, etc.) Each remedialist will want to get acquainted with both the modes and the elements, as this will aid in the suggestion of both symbolic substitutions and remedies.

Inconjunct = 150 degrees

Example: Sun 5 Virgo + Mars 5 Aquarius

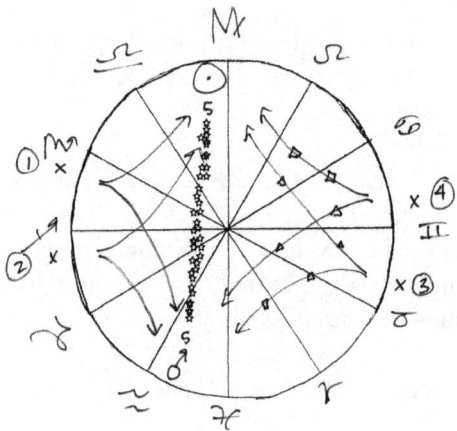

The inconjunct is an interesting aspect, as it creates a rubbing kind of tension between the emissions of the planets. This is not the same kind of intense surging that comes from the square, yet the inconjunct is also less harmonious than the trine or sextile. The reason for this is mathematically quite simple. Because an inconjunct is 150 degrees in separation, there will be times when a transiting planet hits one by a sextile or trine, and simultaneously hits the other by a square. In this combination of transiting activations, one angle is pleasant and the other is difficult. Thus the rub. One thing is going smoothly, while another thing is causing problems.

This can at times create a feeling of guilt in some people. They can't tend to figure how to rectify two seemingly incongruous needs. Here is the mathematical breakdown of the transits to the inconjunct represented on the previous page.

1. 5 Scorpio
2. 5 Sagittarius
3. 5 Taurus
4. 5 Gemini

As we can see, an inconjunct is only doubly activated four times in one planetary cycle. In this manner, it mimics a square in frequency, but in intensity, the internal chaos seems to be less heightened.

Notice that in the example above, one planet is in a *mutable earth* sign (Sun in Virgo) and the other is in a *fixed air* sign (Mars in Aquarius). These two planets are in signs that share little in common, which is also why the inconjunct (and semi-sextile) can create interesting involvements in the lives of people who have them. There are four trigger-points to the natal aspect.

Remedial Considerations: Planets in very different signs are highlighted four times a cycle. The energies are filtered through seemingly-incongruous signs, houses, spheres of life, and parts of the physical and energetic body.

Semi-sextile = 30 degrees

The semi-sextile functions in a similar manner to the inconjunct. Let us take a look at the mathematics of the aspect.

Example: Sun 5 Virgo + Mars 5 Libra

A traveling planet will touch both planets at the following points:

1. 5 Sagittarius
2. 5 Capricorn
3. 5 Gemini
4. 5 Cancer

As we can see, the semi-sextile behaves in exactly the same manner as the inconjunct. Both planets are triggered exactly four times in the cycle; the rhythm being two signs in a row, twice throughout the pattern. Again the feeling is that of a rubbing, irritating struggle, and when remediating both planets must be addressed.

Notice also that the signs of Virgo and Libra are right next to one another, but they are very different in nature. Libra is *cardinal air* while Virgo is *mutable earth*.

Remedial Considerations: Planets sit in signs that are right next to one another, and are highlighted four times in any planetary cycle. The two energies are expressed into two seemingly incongruous signs, houses, spheres of life, and parts of the energy-body that are right next to one another.

Aspects: Case Study

Problematic Aspect: 4 Year Old Child

Natal Saturn *opposed* Neptune
Transiting Saturn in Libra, *sextile* Natal Saturn, *trine* Natal Neptune

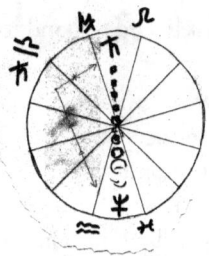

*Transiting **Saturn** ignites natal **Saturn/Neptune** opposition*

Planetary Symptomology:

Emotional: *Scared and confused.*

Experiential: *Seeing animals in basement that other people can not see. Adults tell the child that the animals are not there. This causes distress in the child.*

Behavioral: *Mentions having "problems with her imagination." Afraid to go in the basement.*

Mental: *Struggling to understand what is real and what is not. Trying to define reality.*

Saturn needs: The need to feel the limitations of incarnation, survive within institutions and shared realities, evolve and improve, create boundaries, create structure, have internal feelings of separation from others, feel constriction, experience stress, and manifest a better life.

Neptune needs: The need to sleep and snuggle, channel art and music, merge with others, experience magic and miracles, feel inspired, seek divinity, seek transcendence, attend to the psychic and spiritual self, and respond to vibrations.

Analysis: We know a few things about the nature of this struggle in the entire scope of the life, as we know the tendency of the opposition itself. Throughout this child's life, the energies of Neptune and Saturn will always mix, and the mixings will be triggered 8 times in any one planetary orbit. We know that the angle here will need to be managed.

The planet of Saturn is very concerned with what is real, conforming us to normalized behaviors and ideas. Neptune is more concerned with magic and imagination. The Saturn needs in this chart are expressed in the sign and house opposite to Neptune. This can present through circumstances in which the two soul-needs might seem to be mutually exclusive. We can bridge the two seemingly opposing needs, by honoring the values of both. We can direct energies to spheres of life into which they are wanting to flow. Often children can benefit during Saturn/Neptune periods from language markers such as "real" and "pretend."

Mom, Be a porcupine! Pretend.

*Mom, I want to be a ladybug. For Real!
For Halloween!*

Mom, I am pretending to be a mountain climber!

Mom, I really saw foxes in the basement.

Possible Remediations: Building trust between the parent and child through belief in what the child is experiencing, bridging the real/pretend language gap, asking questions without judgement, asking the child to draw pictures of what they see, asking the child to tell stories about what they see. Teaching the child how to ask for divine assistance in times when they are scared, playing beautiful music to soothe the child (Neptune problems can often be helped by music).

Remedial Technique

15

Symbolic Substitution

Step One: *Discover the Vibratory-Self*

Get to know your chart. Honestly.

Step Two: Make a move towards *Consensual Emission*

Super-express your chart. Awesomely.

The basic premise behind symbolic substitution is the *substitution* of hard planetary energies with easier or more fruitful expressions of the vibrations. We might best approach this topic with a metaphor. Suppose there is a river that is gushing strongly right into the foundation of our house. This will of course deteriorate the structure under which we live. Symbolic substitution would be the act of re-routing this river so that its inherent power can do some good work in our life, as opposed to causing stress and strain. While it might require a bit of effort and time to re-route the river, the benefit in the end will be obvious.

Each planet symbolizes a certain energy in the life, and there are many ways to handle, wrangle, or use the energy of each planet. Suppose a child keeps getting overheated, which leads to behavioral outbursts. Now suppose that we discover the problematic planet to be an extremely hot Mars. While certain remedial techniques will focus on cooling off or neutralizing the overheated Mars, symbolic substitution works to provide an alternate outlet for the vibration. We can often find great success in channeling the heat through introducing a new activity into the life. In the example of the overheated child, we could begin by asking ourselves any of the following questions:

What would be a non-problematic use of the ultra-hot energy of Mars?

Is there an activity that would allow the energy of Mars to be expressed without hurting anyone?

Is there a use of Mars that would not be disgraceful or frustrating?

Is there a use of the heat that would lead to vitality and health?

Is there an use of the Mars-passion that would lead to a better world?

Is there use of the Mars that would be joyful?

In order to truly match the vibrational nature of the child's Mars, we will also want to consider the sign and house placement.

Let us look at the steps in this process.

Symbolic Substitution: The Process

Step One:

Watch the problematic vibration in real time.

Once we have located a planet or aspect that we want to analyze and dissect, through a simple study of the *Ephemeris,* we can look to see when certain planets will be hitting the natal planet that we will be analyzing. The first step in becoming the most high-minded version of our chart is to watch our aspects emerge in real time.

If we have a particularly strong cluster of planets at the same degree, we will want to observe a few transits to this part of the chart and notice our inner feelings, as well as the affect on our physical body, behaviors, and personal relationships.

Step Two:

Observe and document the current expression of the planet.

Once we have found a planet or aspect that we want to analyze further, we can then watch the inner planets (the Sun, Moon, Mercury, Venus, and Mars) trigger the aspect. We should especially observe these aspects when the Moon is also hitting the planet(s), as these moments will produce a pure expression of the planet or aspect that is being ignited. We will then want to observe and document the experience of the natal energy for ourselves.

What happens when Mars and the Moon hit my natal aspect?

What does it feel like when Venus hits the same aspect?

Does the Sun highlight the energies? If so, how?

What happened six years ago when Jupiter and Saturn both sat on the natal aspect?

Does that experience somehow apply to this one?

When Mercury hits the aspect, am I talking about this part of myself?

If so, what is the narrative I am building?

Step Three:

Institute certain remedial measures and observe the effects.

If we find in our research that there is a part of ourself that we would like to manage better, we can begin trying to find appropriate activities for that aspect of our personality. It may take a while to find the right match, so we will want to notice if the substitution is producing the effect we want. If not, see step four.

Step Four:

Adjust accordingly until the appropriate match is found.

At times, a particularly challenging aspect will require a highly creative outlet. We may even want to incorporate a variety of outlets for the same hard vibration. This is a handout I use during workshops where we learn how to watch our own charts emerge in real time. The key is to time inner and outer transits to aspect clusters, and notice when the Moon is also picking up the aspect and triggering the action.

Astrological Self-Portrait

Step One: Analyze the Ascendant sign

> This is the role that you will play in all realms
>
> This shows the general trajectory of your life
> stable/unstable
> Strong personality traits
> The Greeks use a ship analogy

Step Two: Analyze the planet ruling your Ascendant sign

Sign	Ruler
Aries	Mars
Taurus	Venus
Gemini	Mercury
Cancer	Moon
Leo	Sun
Virgo	Mercury
Libra	Venus
Scorpio	Mars
Sagittarius	Jupiter
Capricorn	Saturn
Aquarius	Saturn
Pisces	Jupiter

> This is the pilot of your ship--what is he/she doing?
> House/sign/aspects

Step Three: Look for any of the following

1. Stellium of planets--a cluster of planets in one sign
2. Very tight conjunctions--planets on top of one another
3. Planets in the first house--strong personality indicators
4. Interesting chart configurations; a bunch of planets at the same degree, no tight aspects, insanely tight aspects, all water signs, etc.

Step Four: Write and write about your chart

Step Five: Watch your chart unfold in real time

Step Six: Keep track of your energies through journaling/pictures/video, etc.

Step Seven: Pinpoint parts of your chart that are not "working" for you and try to make them more awesome through remedial measures or symbolic substitution

Step Eight: Keep a record of what does and does not work

Step Nine: Go with what works

Step Ten: Be super mega awesome

Symbolic Substitution: Example

In the case of a conjunction between Mercury and Saturn, we are trying to remedy the problematic cycle of our client having extremely self-critical thoughts. Through research, he has documented that his fears and insecurities get triggered upon every transit to the Mercury/Saturn conjunction.

Mercury/Saturn Conjunction:

If we are to truly substitute the entirety of the vibrational symbology, we must look at the tendencies of both Mercury and Saturn.

There are two ways to approach a planetary aspect in reference to symbolic substitution. One method is to examine the combined vibrational qualities of the two planets involved. Let us call this the *vibrational qualities* approach. In reference to this text, we can examine the combination of vibrations by simply combining the vibrational qualities of the two planets.

The second method is to take a *soul-needs* approach. In this technique, we can simply combine the needs of each planet in an aspect. This can help us find activities that fill these needs.

Vibrational Approach

Mercury vibrations: Fast, active, cerebral, synaptic, lingual, cognitive, perceptive, integrative, processive, frenetic, expressive, narrative-building, filtering, and disclosive.

Saturn vibrations: Tightening, constricting, dense, heavy, cold, pressurizing, stressing, structuring, focused, constructive, solidifying, limiting, congealing.

Mercury + Saturn: Active tightening, cerebral cooling, synaptic constriction, lingual pressure, cognitive focus, integrative limitation, a congealed filter, etc.

Symptomology: The person tends towards excessive creation of mental patterns, which presents an overly exacting mind. The ability to communicate is affected, as the person becomes mentally fearful, obsesses over negative thoughts, etc.

When we look at this combination, we can certainly see a need for astral healing. The vibrational urge of the soul to communicate and to condense will happen all at the same time. Because this combination of qualities is found to be causing problems in some area of the life, we will want to attempt to find ways in which to manage the seemingly competing energies. Some ideas are listed on the following page, but the possibilities are limitless. As noted in the steps above, if one activity is not quite right, we can try another!

Mercury/Saturn: *Symbolic Substitutions*

1. Communicating through the written word, which allows the time and patience to work with the condensing vibration of Saturn. This would also provide distance and time to communicate in one's own distinct way.

2. Communicating the needs in a second, third, or fourth language, bringing an inherent separation and limitation to the ability to communicate. This would provide an outlet for the cerebral stress that is not personal nor emotional.

3. Literally cutting off the ability to communicate so that the person can think in a distinct and separate way from those around him. One way to do this would be for the person to wear noise-canceling headphones. In a partnership, this might mean laying in bed silently, or waiting until the transit is over to discuss a problem. Mercury's need to cogitate is honored here, as is the need for constriction and structure.

4. Taking the word and narrative very seriously, as it is the structural backbone to the life. Making a point to keep all promises, say only exactly what is meant, refine the language, and strive to communicate better. This idea might focus the concretizing thoughts towards healthy outcomes.

5. Write small, everyday contracts with the partner, as these are concretizing communications.

Case Study: Symbolic Substitution

Problematic Configuration:

> Mars in the twelfth house at 24 Gemini
> Venus conjunct the Ascendant at 23 Cancer

Symptomology:

> Cheating.
> Sorrowful sexual circumstances.
> Reading the lover's journal.
> Sorrow over the need for variety in love.

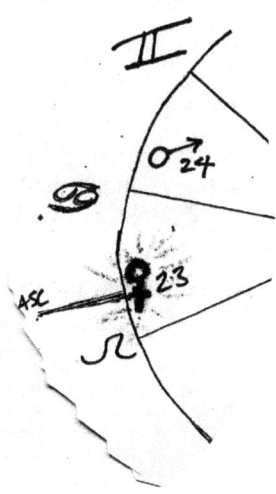

Venus rubs up against Mars in the twelfth!

Analysis of the Energy that is being Fulfilled/Channeled:

Mars in the Twelfth House: The soul has a need for hot experiences in private. Mars brings a hot, impulsive energy to private affairs that might be connected with language and communication (Gemini).

Venus in the First House: The need to commune through the self, to connect in every sphere, to bond through the physical body. The need to be appealing, to give and receive sweetness, the need for adoration, the need to glow and emit beauty.

Analysis: Because Mars is in the twelfth house, there might be attempts to suppress the energy, or deny that the needs of Mars. We are examining the sign of Gemini here, and when the natal chart gets a dose of martian heat, the energy will come in through the throat, arms, hands and chest, as these areas are all connected to the sign of Gemini.

This is obvious from watching transits to natal Mars, as this particular person has consistently written the private thoughts down in a journal; an activity that requires use of the arms and hands. This individual is most likely seeking experiences that bring interest, variety, language, ideas, and stimuli through the twelfth house. Privacy and clandestine operations might be perfect remediations for a twelfth house Mars. In this case, these operations must also involve the use of the mind, or the energy of the planetary placement will not be entirely fulfilled. Because Mars is at the same degree as Venus (in the sign of Cancer), the remediation will be even more effective if it also accounts for the needs of Venus in the first house.

For example, if she is writing erotica, it might be satisfying to also include a "hot mom" theme, as this is an appealing version of a Venus in Cancer. Crafts could be used in any secret Mars in the 12th house operation, such as in the case that the Mars were to be used to make "secret projects." Listed below are just a few possible activities that might provide an outlet for these two combined energies.

Possible Symbolic Substitutions: Writing erotica in private, writing in the journal about secret sorrows, playing an instrument in private, altering the beauty of the arms and hands through the use of needles (getting tattoos), engaging in activities that give use to the arms and hands (which is crucial for a troublesome planet in Gemini). Writing letters to inmates or other people in seclusion, taking secret photos of the arms and hands, baking cakes in the shape of words, or writing letters for a good cause (12th house can be altruistically used).

Putting Symbolic Substitution to the test:

Secret Envelope Show Number One:
Sun, Mercury, Venus, and Mars = Scorpio

Having been amazed at the extreme accuracy of astrology in describing people's personality characteristics, I began to wonder if I wasn't just *literalizing* the transits. What I mean by this is that I wanted to make sure that I was not writing the language of astrology upon events. Instead, I wanted to test the workings of the astral forces as just that; forces that act upon us through some mechanism unknown to our own selves. Moreover, I wanted to test the ability of astrology to predict things in the future without also *informing* that future. I wanted to understand whether I as the astrologer was manifesting the future by talking about that future, or whether the astral energies act upon us whether we are paying attention or not. In the fall of 2010, I noticed something interesting would be happening in the sky. Within a three month period, Venus, Mars, the Sun, and Mercury would all travel through the same portion of the zodiacal sign of Scorpio.

I developed an idea to test the workings of astrology. I scoured my notebooks of charts to find friends who had planets in angles to the 10th degree of Scorpio. I found a number of people willing to participate, and designed an experiment. I opened up my *Ephemeris* and found exact dates and times during which each participant's planets would be ignited by both the transiting inner planets and the Moon.

Hypothesis: The planets act upon us vibrationally when we are not aware of what is happening in the astral schematic.

Research Design: Examine various astral energies as the Sun, Mercury, Venus, and Mars, travel through the same sign of Scorpio in a short period of time.

Astral Energies Examined:

Scorpio Rising: *Uranus 14 Scorpio, Sun 12 Taurus*

This project is found on page 208. The artist, Misti M. made an eclectic poem collage about anxiety and being fidgety, yet doing the right thing nonetheless. The presentation was lo-fi, electric, and poetic.

Taurus Rising: *Saturn 10 Scorpio*

This project is found on page 205-206 The artist, Amber R. made a beautiful hand-embroidered piece about her Saturn experience. The presentation was beautifully hand-crafted, and the medium is timeless.

Gemini Rising: *Mars 10 Virgo*

This project is included on page 207. The artist, Haley W. collaborated with her husband on a durgy musical homage to Mars. Not only did she write a song for Mars, Haley also wrote a piece to go with her song, looking into the particulars of Mars, and made a red paper mache platform for her Mars music video to be played during the show. Well done!

Aquarius Rising: *Uranus 4 Scorpio, Jupiter 9 Taurus*

Visual artist and designer Groshong E. made a multi-media self-portrait to study this opposition in his chart. He documented his energies which he then transformed into a highly stylized digital video. Beautiful merging of Uranus technology with a true eye for beauty!

Libra Rising: *Mars 10 Virgo, Mercury 11 Pisces*

Artist Dar R. made a beautiful hand-drawn and hand-written children's book. The drawings were phenomenal and the story line was magical yet also rhythmic, having been derived from another popular children's story.

Methodology: Each artist agreed to make art on the dates and times during which their specific planets was being highlighted. The medium was entirely up to the artist. The only instructions given were to express the energies in the most natural fashion, whatever they might be. Participants were unaware of what was happening in their astrological charts during the assigned dates and times. Their only knowledge was that they were to express what they were feeling in the times allotted.

The Envelope Project Show

September 25, 2010 = Venus 10 Scorpio
September 30, 2010 = Mars 10 Scorpio
October 20, 2010 = Venus 10 Scorpio (*rx*)
October 27, 2010 = Mercury 10 Scorpio
November 3, 2010 = Sun at 10 Scorpio

December 17, 2010 = Venus 10 Scorpio (*direct*)

Natal Planet: Saturn at 10 Scorpio

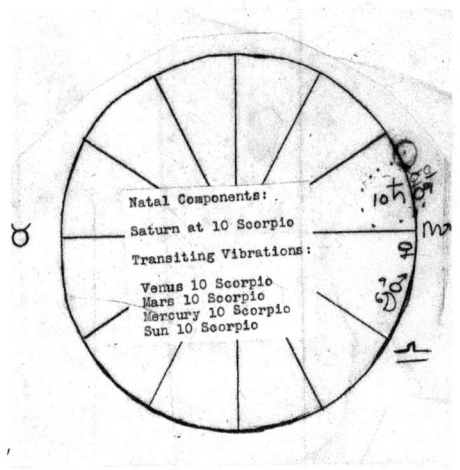

Amber R. channeled the energies of Saturn into art.

The Sun, Mercury, Venus, and Mars
trigger natal *Saturn at 10 Scorpio.*

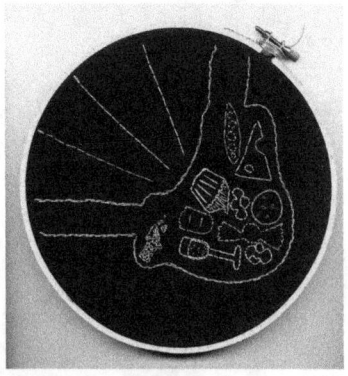

22   THIS IS MY STOMACH ON SNACKS

Basically, my astrological predictions were about Saturn drop-kicking my heart and stomach. I chose to focus most on my stomach because it was more prone to humor, I mean serious art.

This piece represents the day that my girlfriend and I drove from Portland to Vancouver B.C. We ate a lot of snacks. I mean, a lot. Mostly junk food, which isn't unusual, and not really a lot of water. Anyhow, the result was a gut buster. A really terrible tummy-ache right after crossing the Canadian border and getting stuck in traffic while needing to pee.

                Thanks Saturn. Thanks alot.   *by Amber R.*

Artist's Statement:

This project involves video and audio, as well as paper mache and painting. I also created the cloak that envelops the project, at an earlier date. Everything was conceived in a purposeful spirit of chaos and intuition, letting the forces of the Universe guide my actions. Did my experiences match what the secret envelopes said would be happening? Honestly, it is difficult to know exactly, but I will say that on the day that I had the "highest" energy transit-wise, I had a cluster of intense, spiky relational moments (The Harsh Critique was recorded that day), that luckily subsided by later that week.

Mars 15 Virgo, 4th House: Mars can symbolize passionate impulse and action, and is usually conceptualized as male energy, which is something that I'm not sure how I feel about. Mars in Virgo can bring a more nuanced, measured and systematic approach to pursuing ambitions, which does resonate with me lately. Virgo can contain Mars' energy but this I believe can produce anxiety, which physical exercise is really good for. Later when Mars and Mercury were close, it was supposed to enhance my communication, which I'm not sure happened, though on the day the Sun was supposed to be ruling my ego, self, body, and identity, I did find it very easy to connect with people.

The Harsh Critique: After a series of relationally triggering moments, I find refuge in a PSU bathroom stall.

Cheshire Larry David: Irreverence, darkness, goofiness, a curious mix of optimism and cynicism, a sense of randomness, the confidence to just be you, even with all your idiosyncrasies, which could be perceived as flaws.

Mother Mars: We write this dirge melody to pay homage and celebrate the effects of Mars. Mars isn't just a dark, war-like planet, but one that gives emotional resonance and depth, even if uncomfortable, to life circumstances. I prefer to gender-fuck-up astrology because what does "male" energy really mean? I have been conditioned to see male as something that exists outside of me, and even as I rebuff that idea, it is still a roadblock to really experiencing Mars in all her glory. For me. My partner, whom I collaborated with for the song and video, said something cool, which was that Mars evoked "possibilities" for him, because of its proximity to Earth, and potential for life or colonies there. I like thinking of Mars that way, because even destructive or "dark" energies can eventually give way to new opportunities that wouldn't have existed without some kind of preceding break down.

23

---

[23] This artist, Haley W. was documenting the effects of the Scorpio travelers upon her natal *Mars at 15 Virgo*. She also wrote a dark metal song with her now husband in homage to Mars. During the show, her project was on display, along with a red paper mache sculpture to also honor and represent Mars. Her project was phenomenal!

BEING IN CLASS MAKES ME NERVOUS.
I MUST REMEMBER NOT TO TWITCH.

I HAVEN'T BEEN SLEEPING.

I CAN'T CONCENTRATE ON ANYTHING.

I NEED TO WALK MORE. MOVING MY BODY HELPS MY MIND.

I AM HERE NOW- WITH THIS WORLD AND MYSELF.
ALERT.
I WILL DO WHAT I AM SUPPOSED TO DO.

24

---

[24] Artist Misti M. documents the effects of the Scorpio planets on Uranus.

Natal aspect: *Uranus 14 Scorpio opposed to Sun 12 Taurus.*

There exists a second layer to the first *Secret Envelope Project Show*. Not only did I secure specific dates and times on which participants would make their art, I also sent out a packet of secret envelopes to each participant. The contents inside were a series of 5-10 smaller envelopes (depending upon the exact configuration of the chart), each one with a date and time written on the outside. These envelopes were timed to be opened just after the dates and times for making art were scheduled.

Inside each envelope, I had written what would be happening in the time period just before. This of course is referring to the time during which the participant was to be creating art (or documenting their exact feelings and interactions to be portrayed later through art). The point of this was to prove that the predictions about what might be happening were set up *before* the art was to be made. I was also curious to see if each of the participants was in fact feeling the energies of the transits, even if they were not expressing these feelings outwardly.

When the show turned out to be a success, in relation to both research and crowd appeal, I decided to keep on with the envelopes. I began to wonder how pre-timed envelopes could help and heal, and in what ways this might be possible. I began to do more individualized projects with people one-on-one, in order to teach them about their own charts, to solve problems, or to provide magic and mystery. Whatever the reason, the envelopes have won the hearts and interest of many. Since branching off into more specific projects with people, I have attempted to help and heal in a number of situations.

On the night of the first *Secret Envelope Project Show*, I knew that I had convinced myself of something very important. The planets do in some way act upon and through us, even when we are not aware of it. The art projects were each very apt to the energy being examined.

Looking back, I do believe that the show is something that I would like to re-examine. In future research, I would attempt to ensure that participants have zero information about their chart throughout the artistic process. This would block any language from being put upon the energies by an outside influence, and would thus allow for true energetic funneling.

It was also through the process of doing this show that I have come to really understand the possible workings of symbolic substitution. If the astral energies truly do flow into us, then we can point them in any number of directions!

The basic premise of an envelope project, is to work with the timing mechanism of astrology, in order to encourage optimal channeling of certain energies. An envelope project, is the facilitation of symbolic substitution in real time, by use of the US Mail.

Symbolic Substitution:
Consideration

On the need for
Passive and Active Channels
for intense configurations

It is important to understand that the manner in which society is constructed does not always allow individuals to express the energies that come into them naturally. Most institutionalized arenas value the experience of calmness and the facade of similarity. Institutions are not always bad in and of themselves, it is only the labeling and rigidity that occurs within them that can cause problems for those individuals attempting to navigate such rigid structures.

In the case that we are trying to remediate an intense energy in an acceptable manner, we can employ any number of both active and passive remediations.

An *active remediation* is anything that funnels an energy outwards into an action-oriented activity.

A *passive remediation* is anything that satisfies the internal craving, yet does not channel that craving into direct action.

Let us examine this concept through a few examples.

Passive and Active Remediation

Example One

Mars + Neptune

Mars needs: The need to be passionate, instigate, roughhouse, sweat, rage, contend, move fast, and express the internal animal instincts.

Neptune needs: The need to sleep and snuggle, channel art and music, merge with others, experience magic and miracles, feel inspired, seek divinity, seek transcendence, attend to the psychic and spiritual self, and respond to vibrations.

Active: Practicing martial arts, live action role play, playing *Dungeons and Dragons*, vigorous swimming, making perfumes or mixing scents, alchemy, thai chi, sexual role playing, energetic manipulation through qi gong, acupuncture, costume-making, or drawing anime characters.

Passive: Watching martial arts movies, reading about energy work, taking pictures of one's rash (a common Mars/Neptune affliction), using flower essences for inflammatory problems, listening to goth/industrial music, reading about drug-related injuries, or practicing reiki.

Example Two

Mars + Pluto

Mars needs: The need to be passionate, instigate, roughhouse, sweat, rage, contend, move fast, and express the internal animal instincts.

Pluto needs: The need to die and be reborn, take it to the limit, attach the soul to something, be transformed entirely, transmute, become unrecognizable to oneself, go deep, and be drastically and forever changed.

Active: Manipulating clay, soapstone, or other dense materials. Heating and melting things such as through welding or metal fabrication. Channeled energetic transformations, such as DNA restructuring or soul retrieval. Intense, warrior like activities, such as cage matches or arm wrestling. Sexual activities that might alter the physical body itself, play piercing, etc.

Passive: Watching intense movies about death, genocide and parasitic flesh eating diseases. Surrounding the self with transformative individuals, internally confronting one's own death, or contemplating healthy obsessions.

Case Study: Active and Passive outlets for a hard aspect within the natal chart; analysis of symptoms and a substitution of the planetary symbology with possible activities.

Problematic Aspect:

> Mercury in the eleventh house at 7 Libra
> Saturn in the eleventh house at 9 Libra

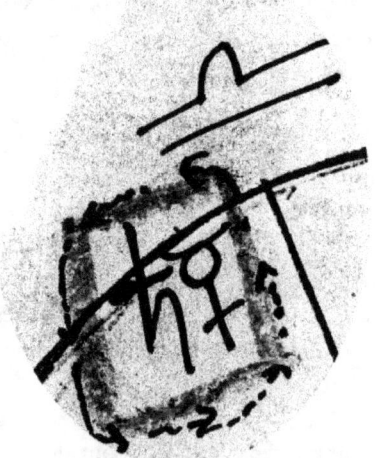

*Mercury/Saturn conjunction
in the eleventh house*

Symptomatic Expressions:

Mental: *Self-hatred, social anxiety in groups, morbid thinking, cyclical thinking, labels placed upon the mental state; bi-polar, anti-social, etc.*

Physical: *Extreme constriction in the wrist, tendonitis (requiring surgery), locking up of the tendon coming from the thumb.*

Behavioral: *Extreme quietness in groups, walking with the eyes facing downwards, making frequent apologies for the self and the existence, identifying with mental illness diagnoses, etc.*

Circumstantial: *Lack of access to transportation. Sorrow through unreliable sources of transportation. Hard situations with friends and creative projects. Not being able to play music on account of fear combined with physical symptoms.*

Analysis: The energy and intention of Mercury is to communicate, and the intention of Saturn is to block things, slow experiences down, and to cause separations. This means that the intention of the soul here is actually towards communicative separations, a point of learning that must inherently come through the incarnational experience. When the native is forced to be around other individuals during hard transits to her natal Mercury/Saturn, the experience will most likely not lead towards a feeling of love and understanding. Instead, the energy will ask that the native either be schooled by another individual (who in this case is representing Saturn), or have other communicatively separating experiences.

Silence is a very graceful use of these energies, as there is an inherent communicative separation, but not one that is malicious or troublesome in nature. A modern solution is to have physical separation from the individual to which she is talking, such as by talking through skype or through the use of letters. In the case that the person were to use a form of video communication, silence plus typing is a good use of the separative and slowing nature of Saturn.

Possible Remediations:

Active: Reclaiming all labels about the state of the mind through writing or other quiet and more restrained forms of expression (such as through playing the guitar or writing in a journal), taking up a study of psychological theories related to friendship or groups (11th house), finding a mentor in the art of diplomacy, or learning a new language through friendships.

Passive: Silence, privately cataloging musical information (Libra), watching documentaries about long-lasting relationships among people who speak different languages (Saturn rules differences), reading books on equality, conflict resolution, or mediation.

16

Strategic Planning as Remediation

Mars square venus/uranus*****Transits

    Mercury----May 25-28
    Venus------May 28-June 1
    Mars-------June 2-9

Jupiter   ******   Transits

    Mercury & Venus ---- May 15-21
    Mars---------------- May 11-21

Mars sextile Pluto/trine Neptune

    Sun---------April 5-9
    Mars--------April 22-28
    Venus-------May 3-8
    Mercury-----May 2-7

Once we have watched charts and transits in real time, it is easier to know how they *tick*. Some charts are very hard working at times, and then tend to relax heavily. Other people meander throughout life, not flaring up much at all. A person with most of their planets in one sign will be quite focused in their activities. A chart with planets scattered throughout will bring about a life that is more haphazard.

By becoming aware of our own patterns, we can then attempt to work with the natural influxings of planetary energies. If the upcoming year will be heavily influenced by Saturn, we will want to prepare to work hard and be schooled. If Jupiter will be prominent, we will have the natural urge to expand, and thus, it might be more of a year for growth. Mars periods are good for differentiation, while Venus periods are more apt for connection. For persons who have intense chart configurations, strategic planning can be quit helpful in maximizing the life experience.

This is one of the most ancient concepts behind the utility of the astral arts. As Porphyry of Tyre said in 200 AD:

It is necessary to closely observe the conditions of the planets and the fixed stars near to them, so that one might keep the fields and the ships and the plants safe and secure. This is not unlike the way in which animals prepare themselves for the winter by finding a calm place to lie motionless and warm, awaiting the chance to move to another more bountiful location when the weather warms; a place providing sweet smells and plenty of water.

In the most simple terms, there is a season for all things. In a more complex manner, we can plan for our transits in order to maximize our manifestation potential. This is good work for the vigilant, transit watching astrologer.

Suppose we are looking at the chart of an eclectic inventor. Certain days will certainly be better for inventing, while other days are more apt for balancing the checkbook. In general, there are some days when we feel more "out of it," and other days we are more "with it." It is the natural cycle of things to ebb and flow. By using the chart to plan deadlines, we can maximize the efficient uses of our energies, creating an atmosphere of joy within the confines of the human experience[25].

Strategic Planning through the use of the planets can be as simple as:

Setting deadlines for the ending of Mars/Saturn transits.

Planning important public appearances on good days.

Planning to constrict the finances under Saturn transits.

Planning to go to networking meetings on Jupiter transits.

Re-building structures during Saturn transits.

Doing activities that require gusto on Mars transits.

Planning activities for each day according to the transits.

---

[25] If we are in charge of our own projects, we are best served by planning our deadlines to the true passing of Saturn. At this point, we know we will be onto a new theme!

Sun transit activities: Dressing ourselves well, shopping, going to the make-up counter, getting a haircut, getting our photo taken, branding ourselves.

Mercury transit activities: Writing emails, making phone calls, thinking, writing, making brochures, planning lectures, calling to make purchase orders.

Venus transit activities: Taking clients out to eat, doing artwork to support our goals, shopping, making friends.

Mars transit activities: Being militant, creating situations that involve a positive challenge, embarking on new activities, focusing on situations that produce *eustress* (good stress).

Jupiter transit activities: Networking for our larger goals, taking hold of opportunities, traveling for work, teaching.

Saturn transit activities: Planning for the long term, detailed and focus-driven projects, intense structure, enduring periods of depravation while working towards a goal, re-structuring.

Uranus transit activities: Engaging extreme free will, allowing for the unexpected, working a random structure into the business model, changing activities day-to-day.

Neptune transit activities: Sleeping in, watching movies that are conducive to our highest goal, conceptual activities such as design or poetry, brainstorming.

Pluto transit activities: Re-formatting hard drives, repairing equipment in the office, transforming a business relationship to be more productive, excavation or clearing.

The short list on the previous page is by no means complete. Each chart has distinct aspect clusters, with unique house and sign placements, and will be drawn to different activities.

When the traveling planets hit natal Saturn, the feeling will be more focused and constricting. The placement of our natal Saturn will show what could be called our *focus receptor*. When the transiting planets hit Saturn, we will want to allow space for constriction in the areas of our Saturn. Transits to Saturn are not good for networking and feeling buoyant or optimistic. These times are good for completing tedious tasks, such as emails or contracts. This might mean that we need time alone to work or to think. In another chart, this might be a need for constriction through a coach or teacher. The configurations to and from Saturn, by aspect, must be considered as well. This is true of any planet that we are trying to plan our lives around.

Now let us look at a case study that also took the form of an envelope project. A good friend of mine is self-employed, but has been having a hard time building his business. Because his chart is a bit erratic, we enlisted astrology for some assistance. We attempted to maximize the daily schedule according to his chart and to channel each of his energies into an activity that would produce results for his larger goal; to build his business. I gave him instructions in envelopes, timed to the days he would be working.

Case Study: A friend is a self-employed photographer. He asked this question:

How do I optimize my daily work schedule and build my business through the use of astrology?

Step One: Define the preferred work hours

Mondays: Work with daughter if possible
Tuesdays: Work 10:30am - 6pm
Wednesdays: Work 10:30am-6pm
Thursdays: Work 1-4pm
Fridays: Work 12:00 noon-3:30pm
Weekends: Off

Step Two: Fill in open time periods with activities that would be most conducive to the transits of each particular work shift.

Self-employed photographer:
Prominent Aspect

Sun/Mars conjunction. 12 degrees Leo. Ninth house.

Sun + Mars Conjunction. Same sign. Same house.

Synthesis: Planet(s) + Sign + House + Aspect

Analysis: The need to exist and to be passionate are as one. When the Sun is triggered by transit, Mars is also ignited. Every time! The need to exist passionately is most naturally expressed and understood through hearty joy. The soul has a need to exist passionately through an intense expression of fun and joy. This passion will most naturally be expressed and received through the activities of long-distance travel, higher education, religion, or philosophy.

If we are now wanting to integrate this soul-need into the realm of work, we will want to find activities that will fulfill this need, but will also drive towards a sustainable structure of the business.

Career-focus: Visual media, photography, and film.

Possible long term symbolic substitutions: Travel photography, location scouting, teaching photography at the local college, working in the business of fun, working to brand people (Leo), dressing the self in a daring and individualized manner, styling people, styling the self, working on fun projects.

Possible short-term symbolic substitutions for growth of the business as a whole entity: Networking at conferences, meeting new people and having fun, taking clients out to lunch, being confident, throwing an art show or party, branding the self, making business cards, taking pictures of oneself for materials, designing a brochure about the unique skills and abilities of the business.

Saturn in Taurus. 21 degrees. Sixth house.

Long-term Symbolic Substitutions: Maintaining a family business, being fixed in daily habits that are health-inducing, acquiring and allocating resources, providing a good foundation for one's business.

Short-term Symbolic Substitutions for growth of the business as a whole entity: Doing business taxes, editing photos, paperwork, scheduling appointments, building benches for darkrooms, affixing and allotting resources, focusing on long-term structural needs for the business, building sets.

**Venus/Pluto conjunction.
26 degrees Virgo. Tenth House.**

Long-term Symbolic Substitutions: Having an art-based career, communing and becoming transformed entirely through a precision-oriented process which is also servile in nature. Being a photographer for architectural clients. Small scale beautifying of individuals through portraiture.

Short-term Symbolic Substitutions: Taking beautiful and crisp photos of public places, having art shows, photo shoots in public, meeting and interviewing models, transforming a room into a photo or video set, having meetings about art direction, developing beautiful prints to be shown in public, taking large-scale architectural shots.

17
Astral Loving:
Vibrational Merging as Remediation[26]

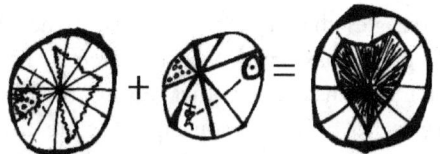

[26]

The information in astrological charts can be used to help us understand relationships and avert possible disaster. In fact, a simple check of a *theoretical composite chart* can often avert heartache, sexual incompatibility, violence, and abusive patterns. We do not want to guide people seeking a successfully free and open sexual relationship into a composite with a hard Mars/Saturn aspect. We also do not want to merge into a composite business, in which the chart indicates severe communication blockages. We can also check composites in order to attempt to partner up with someone who can naturally be uplifting in our areas of weakness. Perhaps we were born with a Mars/Saturn connection, which has proven to be quite frustrating. Compositing into a Mars/Jupiter conjunction might allow us to express a part of ourselves that we generally cannot.

Astrology as a whole can help maintain good relationships, in that an examination of the charts can help couples know when relationship struggles will be over, which can provide solace in times of conflict. This information might even allow individuals to agree to not break up until certain harsh energies pass. Astrology can help couples and families understand their cycles and successfully plan activities, such as when to take family trips, when to work a lot, when to take a risk, etc. In this chapter, we will focus on the technique of *intentional compositing* as a remedial measure for natal strife. When dealing with hard and persistent natal aspects, it is quite useful to use composite energies to aid in releasing certain struggles that have existed within the life for many years. If a person has experienced an extremely hard childhood or is extremely sensitive for other reasons, then it will be even more crucial to be in relationships that are conducive to a brighter future. Let us begin with a few assumptions.

Axiom Number One:

> It is possible to minimize time spent hanging around people with whom we meld poorly.

Axiom Number Two:

> It is possible to maximize happiness by engaging in beneficial and uplifting relationships.

In non-astrological terms, we could say that it is beneficial to hang around people who inherently make us feel good. What the composite chart will indicate is how two people will feel if they are to merge with one another over time. When we think of merging, we often think of partnership in the marriage sense. But energetic merging can happen in a number of ways. The process of merging into a composite chart requires time, attention, and the sharing of needs, wills, desires, and language. Moreover, there exist many transits between a first meeting and a complete merging. The length of time it really takes for two individuals to truly merge depends of course on the two people involved.

If two people live far apart from one another, the process of "compositing" could take much longer, and may not truly occur until the two people move in together. The astrology itself can play a role as well. If both individuals in a relationship have a natal Moon/Neptune conjunction, then the composite chart will have a Moon/Neptune conjunction. The compositing will be very quick, as both individuals will be very sensitive to energetic changes.

If both people have a natal Moon/Saturn conjunction, it might prove difficult to get together in the first place. Both partners will approach the relationship with rigid emotional boundaries, meaning that they might both be too cool to warm up to one another in the first place. If these two individuals did in fact end up on a date, such as through internet dating or whatnot, the emotional mixing might also feel cold.

When attempting to merge into higher energies, it is important for people to understand that merging is a process. Any time a new relationship enters our life, it takes time to mutually alter the thought structures and paths of both people involved. Moreover, the combined wills of the two individuals will require a new narrative to be created and attached to the new selves and the relationship. If the composite chart between two people is good, it could be said that the mutual intentions of the two individuals are compatible. If the composite chart is challenging, then it will be hard for two people two vibe well together.

The manner in which each person experiences a relationship has a great deal to do with the transits. The health of the couple as a unit will often come under scrutiny during periods of testing. When a composite chart is positive, loving, and accepting, a bad transit will often be interpreted by a couple as circumstantial stress. Most likely, outside circumstances will be blamed for the hard energies, as opposed to the relationship itself. A harmonious relationship will aid the two people involved as they experience both the positive and negative circumstances throughout life.

In the case of a harder composite chart, the relationship can often be blamed and scrutinized during difficult periods. Then, when Jupiter periods enter the life, the couple re-unites with the idea of the relationship as a positive force. Most simply, hard relationships make everything else a bit more challenging. In order to assess the health of our relationships, we do not inherently need to look at the composite chart. We can instead ask ourselves a number of practical questions about the outcome of being with our partner.

Is this partnership conducive towards a mutually positive future? Are my girlfriend and I fighting to become better people? Do my lover and I believe and trust in one another's highest intentions? Does my relationship build me up or bring me down? Does this business partner make me feel like doing successful business? Am I able to easily thrive in this situation?

If we have asked ourself these very practical questions, we can then also look to the composite chart to examine the potential of a complete pair-bonding of the two charts. The composite chart can in some ways be thought to represent the *molecule* made between two people. Thus, the more energy two people put towards collaborating together, the more the composite chart will express itself in the lives of both individuals. It is also important to notice that each composite chart has its own strengths, weaknesses, and interests. Each composite chart is a fascinating combination of energies. Some couples are better at communicating than others, while some combinations make great lovers. Some people build large businesses together, while others make babies. Any time we deeply collaborate, we share energies, and different fruits can result from each merging.

It is important to consider the fact that each natal chart has different needs within the realm of relationships as well. For instance, a person with a natal Venus square Jupiter will not do well in a composite chart with a Venus conjunct Saturn. Conversely, a person with a Venus conjunct Saturn in the natal chart might find a composite Venus/Jupiter square to be much too frivolous. As an astrologer, I try never to analyze a composite chart through the lens of what I would want in a relationship, because this is entirely different from what my client's soul might most desire. An earthy person will want some stability within a relationship. An electric type will crave and need an exciting composite chart. If the relationship is lacking in excitement, then it might not withstand the test of a Saturn transit.

We absolutely do not want the same things in a relationship with a business partner as we do with our reiki practitioner. The act of being lovers will require a specific set of energies, while making a book together might require its own composite configurations. It is also important to understand that individuals with energetically sensitive charts will require a good composite chart in successful personal relationships. Vibe-sensitive individuals can often bring idealistic joy to those around them every day. Yet when sensitive people are sucked into bad relationships, the outpouring of love energy gets immediately channeled into trying to save or help the other person or the relationship. If we are analyzing a natal chart in reference to its relationship needs, we must first decide what kind of connection or partner would be the best fit. We can ask ourselves some of the following questions.

Does this chart currently want a high-sex partnership? Does this person want to date a business partner? Does this chart tend towards marriage? Which archetype does this chart covet in love? Does this person want someone who is into sports? What might they want their everyday relationship life to look like? Are they looking for a spiritual partner, with whom they can practice tantra, go to hot springs, and channel love from the maker?

As we analyze the chart in relation to questions like these, we are trying to discern what it is that the soul truly might crave in partnership. Once we have engaged the chart in this manner, either by ourselves or with our clients, we can then take this knowledge into our everyday lives. We can seek out places at which people who fit the optimal idea of a partner might hang out. If we want to take this to the next level, we can "weed the garden" by checking the *theoretical composite chart* with prospective dates, friends, or business partners.

It is important to check the composite chart in the case that we are looking for any sort of long-term happiness through merging. If we are looking for a short term burst of energy or joy to spice up our current situation, such as through a creative relationship or a fling, then an evaluation of the natal and current synastry should suffice.

Observations on Composite Charts

1. If one really wants to learn how to read composite charts with potential lovers, friends, spouses, etc., read Robert Hand's book entitled *Planets in Composite: Analyzing Human Relationships*.

2. If we don't want to accidently composite with someone, it is best to avoid doing the energy-love-mingle, eye-stare, wild-thing with them. Yes, lovemaking is a catalyst to compositing.

3. A "less than desirable" composite chart is forever.

Note: when the partnership is physically or emotionally gratifying in certain ways, this can in fact be hard to accept.

4. If there are struggles in a composite chart, they can be remediated *if and only if* the combined vibration is positive enough to allow such a fix.

5. It is an act of utilitarianism for people to combine into uplifting energies, as the feelings of good cheer associated with happy combinations tend to spill out upon the world around them.

6. If a composite chart has a stressful aspect cluster, the stress will in fact be ignited on transits to the composite chart.

7. The same composite chart could be ideal for one person's natal tendencies, yet be difficult in relation to the other person's needs.

When we engage in the art of *intentional compositing*, there are a few important things to remember. First of all, relationships require effort, and thus, we should plan to settle in for a bit of a bumpy ride. Compositing takes work, and there are a few steps to the process. They are as follows:

Letting go of the old ideas about who we are.

Accepting that a change within us will occur as we "give ourselves" to another individual.

Shedding old memories that hold us back from our new selves.

Integrating the new unit into our existing life structure.

Emerging as a happier and more uplifted version of ourselves.

As we traverse this process, it can be useful to avoid assigning the struggles caused by a bad transit to one chart or the other as a "problem with the relationship." A bad transit is temporary and can exist within one chart, whereas an ongoing problem would clearly be shown from a stressful energy in the composite chart. A good method is to try the relationship out for a set period of time, evaluating the nature of the relationship under at least one period of planetary duress. If we like how the compositing energies feel, we can keep on with things. At times, the manifestation of the mutual vibration ends up being problematic in some manner. Lastly, we must acknowledge that compositing inherently changes our energetic field. Who we are before we merge with someone is very different than who we are after we merge with them. The level and degree of this merging depends a great deal on the nature of the charts involved.

18

The Art of *Astrally-Timed*

Information, Love, Assignments, Advice, and Assistance

Exact astral timing is one profoundly healing use of astrology. If we assume that astrology is the *study of the quality of time*, then we can use the chart to observe and anticipate our emotions through past, present, or future transits. Because of this amazing ability of the astral arts, we can heal and guide ourselves into balance and joy. On a consulting level, we can use astrology creatively to help people who are experiencing an extreme quality of time. Here is an example of some of the information I ask for when designing an envelope project.

```
When mailing me a question for a single envelope or a proposal
                                  for an art project...
Please Include All of the Following:

    1. Birth Date, Time and Location.

    2. Your street Address

    3. Your Question

    4. Any Clarifying Information About Your Question
       Examples:

       Descriptions of dates and times during which the
            problem has occurred.

       Additional Chart Info (if there is a question about
                           a child, relationship, a date, etc.)

       A Brief History of You, If helpful.

       An Image Of A Similar Project That You Have Made and
            Want to Continue Through Secret Envelopes.

    Anything Else You Want to Send.

    5.    The Signed Consent Form

    6.  A Check or Money Order For the # of
        S.E.s You Want.

        Example: 3 Secret Envelopes    3 x _ = _
    
    7. Anything I forgot to Mention.
```
[27]

---

[27] Information necessary for an astrologer to analyze the chart and conceptualize a *pre-timed Secret Envelope Project*.

During a secret envelope project, the envelope recipient and I have worked together to decide on the goal and structure of the project. Each project is entirely unique, as each astrological chart has its own needs, strengths, and weaknesses. The goal is to help, heal, or honor the highest version of our chart through time-based envelopes, learning, and fun.

The first thing we want to know when designing a project is:

What is our goal?

Are we trying to research something? Are we trying to learn about an aspect-cluster? Do we want to teach a couple about each other's personality aspects in real time? Once we have defined the goal and intent of the envelope project, we can develop our methodology from there. Here are a few ideas, though the options are limitless:

> While the possible uses for pre-timed envelopes are endless, it will be useful to look at some of the past successes.

Addictelopes *were used to remedy a Sun/Moon/Saturn cluster, which was producing eating disorder-like behaviors (pp 320-322).*

Channelopes *were used with a woman who is extremely psychic to the world around her on account of her Mercury square Neptune. She channeled art when the psychic transits were overly harsh, as instructed by pre-timed envelopes (page 243).*

Dommalopes *were used for a man who wanted to learn how to better market his business (221-226).*

Learnalopes were used with a woman in Washington in order to teach her about the different parts of her chart in real time (p 160).

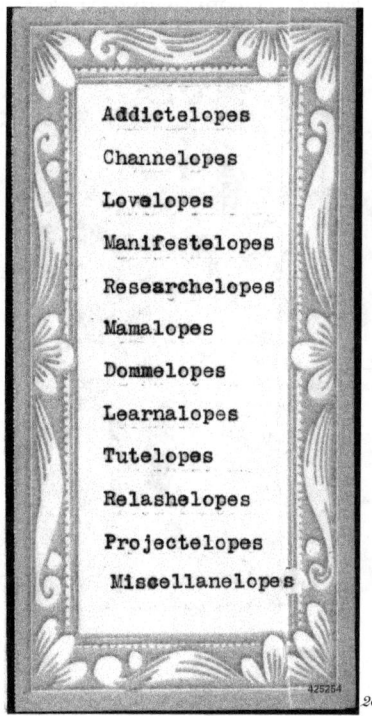

28

---

[28]The exact information included in each envelope depends entirely on the goal of that envelope. If the receiver is needing information, then a tutelope might suffice. In the case that there is *extreme Saturn duress*, a Lovelope might be the best option.

Case Study: Can a person naturally channel creative inspiration on transits to an intense natal Neptune configuration. Can knowing the language of what is happening in the stars lessen the scary feelings of the perceptive specialities that come with hard Neptune aspects?

* * *

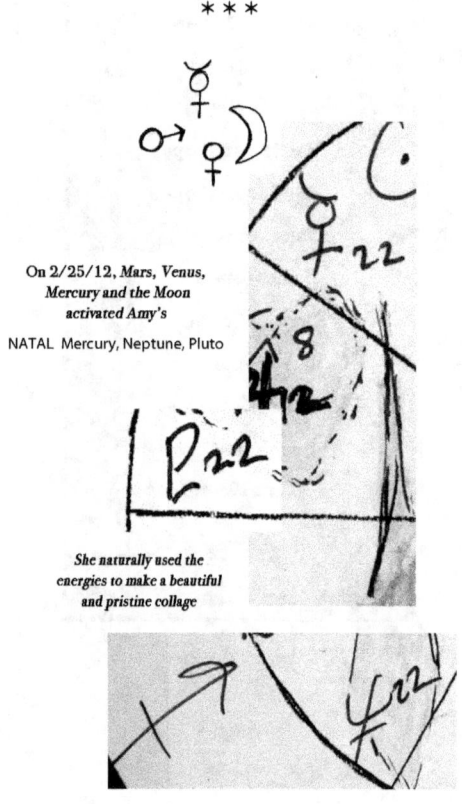

On 2/25/12, Mars, Venus, Mercury and the Moon activated Amy's

NATAL Mercury, Neptune, Pluto

She naturally used the energies to make a beautiful and pristine collage

I sent Amy a packet of envelopes in the mail. We had agreed that she was to open them at certain dates and times, which were written on the outside of each envelope. She would read about what was happening in her chart afterwards. We wanted to try this Astral Art therapy because Amy is an artist, and her mind is very special!

Amy channels Venus, Mars, Mercury & the Moon[29]

---

[29] Amy has an exact natal Mercury square Neptune.

Mercury 21 Virgo   She channeled this beautiful art when
Neptune 21 Sagittarius   Venus, Mercury & the Moon
Pluto 20 Libra   hit the aspect on 2/25/12

Advanced Considerations

19 Is Astrology Inherently Fate-Based? An Interview with *Judith Hill*

World-Renowned
Medical Astrologer
Herbalist
Fairy
Genius
Princess
Mensch

What is your background in Remediation?

My formal astrological studies began at the age of ten. Since the age of fourteen, I've read everything I could about the traditional effects of stones, herbs, colors, sounds, and music. Specifically, I have studied how these things relate to the body, the anatomy, the mind, and the soul of man, as they are mirrored in the astrological birth chart. My focus has been the practical application and expression of the birth chart and its potential use as a diagnostic tool for medical practitioners and psychologists.

I have a "Chartered Herbalist" degree with the *Dominion College of Herbal Sciences*, and have studied and practiced Medical Astrology for decades. I've written ten books including the topical *Medical Astrology; A Guide to Planetary Pathology*, and have developed an independent study course available to medical astrology students[30]. As a lifetime consulting astrologer, I've given now somewhere in the range of 9,000 personal readings, and have invested ten years in the statistically-based scientific research of astro-genetics and astro-seismology.

I've taught classes on "Upaye," a Jyotish remedial technique using stones to antidote planetary conditions in the birth chart, such as in strengthening a planetary deficiency. I've also studied extensively the field of astro-physiognomy, which is the science of the physical expression of the birth chart. Readers may recognize my book called *The Astrological Body*

---

[30] See the end of this chapter for more information about this wonderful course!

Types. Most recently, I've been studying and teaching renaissance medicine and herbal remedials.

This is a rather brief account that should suffice for our purposes here. However, this lifetime of experience is but one grain of sand on the beach. We must keep questioning. The study of astrology is infinite in scope.

What is the connection between Mrs. Winkler and Remediation?

Mrs. Winkler is the main character of my fairy tale book entitled *Mrs. Winkler's Cure,* which I have written under the pen name of Julia Holly.

Mrs. Winkler has a very special telescope that she calls her "anthropomorphoscope," which looks into the hearts and minds of men and women. Mrs. Winkler herself represents an evolved human being living on earth, with her vast knowledge being inclusive of many interesting remedial measures.

What are some of Mrs. Winkler's Remedials?

In chapter one, Mrs. Winkler goes through all of her standard herbal elixirs and herb drawers, but can't find the remedial, because in this particular case, the remedial is a spiritual one. It is nonphysical. The client needs something completely unique to him, which is how remedials work. Ten people each might have a cold, but each one might be given a different remedial, depending on their constitution and unique nature.

This philosophy is similar to Homeopathy, a field of remediation which never treats two people the same, nor labels the disease condition with a "diagnosis." In other words, there exists no "influenza" within homeopathy, but instead there is a group of symptoms recognized for a certain person. This is not to say that I don't recognize disease conditions, because both philosophies can be true simultaneously. I see both sides of this argument as being true. There is an influenza virus that a lab technician can see in a microscope. This is a real thing. But the remedial measure used for each person will depend completely on each unique situation.

Do you think that most physical suffering comes from a problem in the energetic field?

The most simple answer is yes.

Most physical problems will be shown in the natal chart, which tells us that something in the energetic matrix at the birth moment acts to create imbalances that lead to disease. Such as, why is one person always phlegmatic and another person is always skinny? The scientists would say, oh it's their DNA! Astrologers would ask how the birth moment influences the DNA via the turning on and off of the *epigenes*, which influence which genes will be turned on and off after the birth moment. So often, a person physically looks just as they should from their birth chart. Something is going on here above and beyond inherited DNA.

How do Remedials work?

If we are talking about stones or amulets, then a stone can work as a deflector of light, an absorber of planetary light, or a translator or amplifier of planetary light. A stone can even function as a neutralizer of planetary light, or as a protector due to its vibratory frequency. In the case of an amulet or talisman, in which case the remedial is not a stone, then the effects are due to the thought forms involved. This is why the Jyotish in India used stones combined with a ceremonial application of sound and chants to the planets before putting on the stones. In part, the remedial effects here are occurring on account of the thought forms imbued within these stones as well.

So, say you have a situation in which you want to strengthen the Sun, or somebody's heart. You can wear a stone upon the heart or on the fourth finger that will bring in more solar energy. But suppose you have a situation where you are receiving the baleful influence of Saturn and you want to deflect it or neutralize it. In this case you also might want to wear a stone that will absorb or neutralize that bad vibration. Or you can use a stone that will put yourself in harmony with that planet. This is another way of using the stones. Or you can put on a talisman, which doesn't perform either of these functions, but it has a holy word or a symbol from someone who has blessed it, and this thought form then resonates with the subconscious of the person who is wearing it. Such as you wouldn't put a crucifix on a Jewish person, but a blessed crucifix can work serious miracles with a devout Christian.

Some talismans and amulets are mechanical or chemical in their action, and some are due entirely to thought and thought vibration. Or the vibration of the person who has administered the talisman or amulet.

Other kinds of remedials, such as actions to perform, homeopathic remedies, or herbs act in these same ways. They are either counteracting or deflecting, or they can be enhancing or absorbing a vibration that is bothering a system. And we are talking planetary vibrations here. Or, they can introduce an entirely new vibration. If you add one drop of black ink to to a glass of water, the whole glass of water is changed.

You can think of a person and their current condition as being an intricate set of interlocking numbers or vibrations, as vibration is in fact numbers. And then think about introducing one new number to this intricate set of numbers that compose up a person and you could change everything. This is how sometimes you get a miracle cure from something as simple as wearing a ring. Or changing the position of the bed. Or a piece of furniture.

Can all things be "cured" ?

Yes, unless the problem has gone too far. There could be a vibrational or physical remedy for any condition if it can be discovered. There are cases in which a disease has gone too far, however, yet even in such cases remarkable healings have been witnessed. In my opinion, hope is never gone until the expiration of the last breathe.

Are some things totally fated?

Yes.

Can one remediate problems in his or her own chart?

Yes, but this is more difficult because there is the challenge of reading one's own chart correctly.

With remediation, one must be quite inventive and willing to try weird things. A remediation could be something such as wearing a piece of obsidian on your left ankle and exposing yourself to Pachabel's *Canon in D* for one hour each morning. It is astonishing how the correct remedial can heal. Fifty-thousand years of Indigenous Shamanic remedial work wasn't just *Bupkis*[31].

How do you know which Remedial to prescribe?

Well at first you don't know. You first have to study the chart and its condition and then ask appropriate questions and then you might come up with several possible remedials. It is always a bit of a fishing expedition, although some remedials are very traditional for certain problems. And then you have to be very careful and think about it some more, and then wait until you get a prod from the universe. Such as you tell them that maybe moonstone might help with this condition, and they say, "Oh my goodness my grandma just gave me a beautiful giant moonstone necklace." And there is your confirmation.

---

[31] Yiddish for *"nothin', nada, just flat out nothing"*.

And then you want to make sure that the remedial will not cause another problem in the chart. For instance you might help a weak Moon by giving the person more Mars energy, as this can supplement an anemic or depressive tendency. But then you might find that Mars will disturb the person's Sun, and then they all of a sudden have more arguments with their husband. And this is why we are always very careful when suggesting red or blue remedies, as these are the remedies of Mars and Saturn. The human body does not do well when it is either too hot or too cold, red or blue. In fact, most health conditions can be traced back to astrological temperature extremes. Such as the reality that one sibling could get an inflammatory arthritis, yet a sibling who eats the same diet can be free from this malady. You will find too much Mars energy in the afflicted sibling (i.e. red). The same is true with most conditions. You will find either an excess or deficiency of a particular element or planetary energy.

So remedials set out to supply a person with missing energies, or to re-channel excessive energies, or to introduce a third factor to harmonize the energies. Basically you are looking for excesses and deficiencies and finding solutions. In this process, you become an astral mechanic.

Is death a choice?

In some people's cases, certainly. In others, not.

People have variable karma. Some people have flexible karma, living their lives like tumbleweeds. The life is variable in cases such as this. The individual may have several close calls, or may have had several substitutions for death in the metaphorical sense, such as moving all the time. Some people have a fixed moment of death. I have seen cases where death is clearly shown in the chart, yet the person was resuscitated and lived for ten years. Was the resuscitation part of the karma?

We have an idealized version of death in the culture. Some people say death is fixed, so go ahead and run in front of a bus because you are not going to die until your time comes. This is only true in some cases. Why would we do astrology if death couldn't be prevented? We have several possible futures at any given moment.

And sometimes you can see the person as driving too fast towards a cliff. If they stop in enough time they won't go off they cliff and they end up in your office. And you say stop smoking now because in two years from now there will be great danger to your lungs. At that point in time it is still up to them how long they live. Two years later they may not have that option. There are cases that seem...well...both answers are true. Some people's death is fixed, whereas others may not be so ordained.

Tell me about your successes with Neptune Remedial Measures.

Here is a good one. It wasn't a remedial measure, but a discovery of what was wrong with my client. Five different doctors couldn't figure out what was wrong with her, as she was suffering greatly with horrible symptoms and was nearly dying. I saw that Neptune was the culprit and Neptune was in an air sign. I suggested that she was being poisoned through the air. She thought I was nuts. It turned out that some work men came into her home and discovered that she had a carbon monoxide leak and her health quickly recovered after it was fixed.

Sometimes you have to go completely with Neptune and sometimes you have to antidote Neptune. Sometimes the person is wanting to sleep, or stare and do nothing. Their whole being needs to rest. If they do nothing and they don't push themselves, then joy and energy will come back to them. Sometimes people just need to be in a period of hanging in the middle of a hammock. Open any magazine and look at any single photograph with humans in it and you will notice that in our culture, everyone has to be smiling and happy all the time. This is not true in other cultures. Some native peoples do not trust white people because they smile and laugh all the time.

The French people consider constant smiling to be imbecilic. Our culture doesn't understand the concept of doing nothing, which is so necessary under certain Neptune transits. Some forms of depression under Neptune are simply a desire to stop being energetically young and spunky, smiling and ambitious, and exciting, and happy. This "happy happy" expectation in american culture is a great strain on people. Especially women, who are always expected to be smiling. Men are always expected to be ambitious and energetic. If you study Native American cultures, you will find that these expectations do not hold and people don't smile all the time; they are very dignified. However, some Neptune aspects indicate anemia. Anemia, leaks, psychic parasites, or clinical depressions. Disease can be antidoted with remedies suitable to the chart, but especially those of Saturn, Venus, Jupiter, and Mars.

How would you describe the difference between a transiting Neptune hitting Saturn, as compared with a Saturn transit to natal Neptune?

Knowing this difference is extremely essential to the student! Is not a boat moving over a river different in effect from that of a river moving over a boat? The natal planet is a part of the birth imprint, forming a stationary, vibratory entity operating on several levels within the "native" (i.e. the special person who chose this birth moment). The transiting planet is a temporary influence, is moving, and is therefore imparting its influence TO the natal planet. Not the other way around!

For example, transit Neptune acts to dissolve the structure and security of a natal Saturn; whereas transit Saturn inclines to suppress or crystallize the fog like mysticism of a natal Neptune. Results of either scenario can be either positive or negative, depending on the attitude of the native toward the experience of the planets. In the former, we may feel insecure, or suffer from weakening bones. In the later, we may become depressed because our rose colored glasses are broken. Of course, there are positive remedials for these often difficult transits. But do you see? It's an important distinction and we have no business selecting remedials if we cannot grok this point.

There is a very significant difference in any transit-natal planetary conjunction, depending upon what planet is doing the transiting and which one of the pair is natal. This must be understood before attempting to interpret transits. These subtleties must also be grasped before selecting remedials for current transit patterns.

Would you prescribe a different Remediation at the beginning of a long transit, versus the end of the transit?

If there was going to be a long term problem, as in a more serious aspect, I would give remedies someone could use for a long time. For instance, you don't tell a client to use horsetail herb or cayenne everyday, as this might set up an irritation in the urinary tract. For long term influences, we might instead use a remedial such as a stone, stretches, or liniments. You would have to use a remedial that the person could use for a long time. This could even be something such as changing their name for the duration of the transit. In the Jewish religion, one can change the name if the person has been threatened with oncoming death. The acute remedies are preferred for acute conditions.

Do you find it challenging to get people to believe you?

It depends on the person. People who come into my office of their own volition, not so much. Women and gay men are more open to astrology than heterosexual men as a rule. And heterosexual women seem also to be more open to remedials than heterosexual men, as a rule. The average person encountered at a party typically scoffs at anything to do with the word "astrology," which they perceive with a curious array of mental images, mostly to do with the occult and charlatanism. Make no mistake, they view the astrologer as either a well-meaning nutcase or a fraud. My solution to this dilemma is to ask them very politely, "sir, how long have you studied astrology?"

They always say they have no need to study astrology. And I say, learn astrology well enough to calculate and read horoscopes, and then let us have a discussion. Hopefully this is changing. I understand that 50% of Americans believe in astrology. But still, very few people really know what astrology is and what astrologers really can do. The astrological chart is a X-ray machine into all aspects of a human being, of which there is no extant parallel.

What do you know about remediation through Symbolic Substitution? [32]

It works quite well in many cases, however with Mars one must be careful. If you have a violent Mars aspect, such as a Mars/Uranus conjunction coming, I would not necessarily go and outlet this energy at the boxing ring or go riding a motorcycle in heavy traffic. You are likely to have an accident. Let's not be stupid. This is not time to play around with heavy equipment while drunk.

How can one remediate this aspect? We know that there will be a tendency for sudden unexpected muscular releases of tension. First take a look at the life. If the person is prone to muscle strains, they should warm themselves up in the morning and avoid extremes of the muscles. If the person has temper control issues, otherwise known as tantrum management problems, then they should stay away from other people during this transit as they will be volatile. They

---

[32] For more information on Symbolic Substitution, see chapter 15.

should not wear red or eat hot spicy foods as this will exacerbate the problem.

We have two approaches to each remedial. One is to increase the energy of the offending planet which is the theory behind homeopathy. The other method used is to give the antidote to the energy. The question of which to do takes a bit of common sense. You must make a study of the individual client, as a phlegmatic, depressed person will respond to the Mars/Uranus vibration differently than will a hyperactive person. The phlegmatic person may welcome this aspect, and for them I would suggest finally getting off their duff and starting a new exercise program. This transit of Mars will give them the rising up energy to do so. Remediation is an art form, much like delicate cooking. Do they have too little Mars or too much Mars to start with?

For example, transiting Mars on a natal south node is often a dilly. This is no time to be trying to buy cars, run for office, or fix anything.

You tend to lose, so how can one use this aspect to avoid the losses? This is a great aspect for throwing out the garbage or doing volunteer labor, the type depending on the sign it is in. This will mitigate much of the negative karma that gets stirred up with this position. One can also use it to become aware of addictions, and to start to get rid of things that are bad for oneself. However, you have to be careful because Mars can at times indicate that remedials could do harm, including certain medicines that could hurt the native.

So we see that symbolic substitution works in some cases and not in others. The astrologer here must be very inventive so as to come up with a perfect substitution. For instance, suppose that during a transit from Saturn to natal Neptune, you find that your client has become extremely depressed. Morbidly so. You have to dig into your bag of knowledge and find what Neptunian aspiration or creative work this person can put form on (Saturn is form). Is it a musical composition? Is it time to build a perfect peace garden? Why spend your time having your rose colored glasses crushed? Why not do something with your dreams?

My teacher always insisted that any planetary aspect could be shifted to its positive polarity, one must only know how. Of course this is easier said than done.

What do you know about Remediation and children?

Not much, as I don't have children myself. I have found that children do seem to respond more quickly to planetary transits than do adults, however. My opinion is that children also respond more strongly to remedials, from what I've seen. Children in general are more responsive to planetary energies.

How would you remediate heartbreak?

That's a tough question because heartbreak is emotional and not physical. I would probably head for the *Bach Flower Essences*. I would also examine the chart in total, as people are very different in how they handle heartbreak. You have the people who become depressed. And then you have the people who become angry. And both types can of course fly to extremes. Then you have the drinkers, which are the people who tend to want to numb themselves.

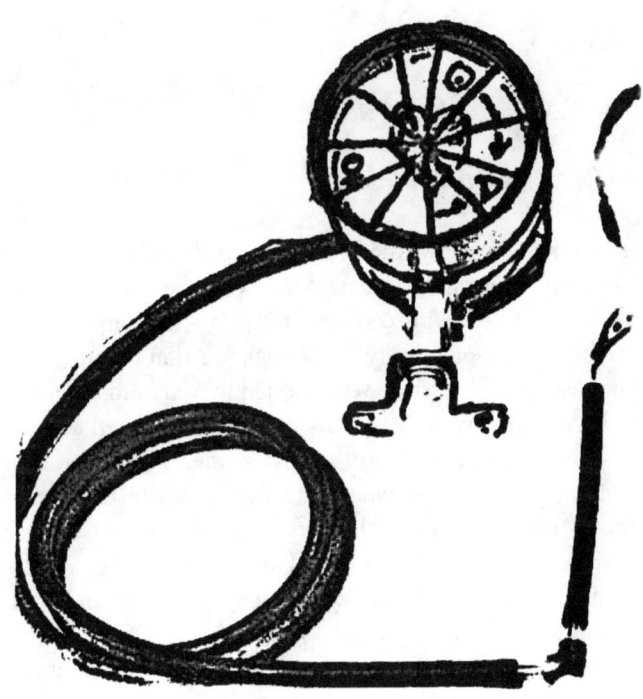

What would you prescribe for a highly unruly Mars, such as in the case that a person had a Mars/Pluto Uranus conjunction in the first house?

Judith: *What sign?*

Andy: *Scorpio*

Judith: *What are the Symptoms?*

Andy: *The case is theoretical*

It depends on how the Mars/Uranus/Pluto is presenting. Normally we would antidote Mars with the Moon, because we antidote heat with coolness. But Mars in Scorpio is wet, and if the person is very emotional, we don't want to use lunar energy. If Saturn is well-aspected to Mars and the person is having an overactive colon or is undisciplined in their emotions by being rude and aggressive, then I would probably look towards a Saturn remedy. I would prescribe this because Saturn is harmonious with Mars in certain contexts because Mars is exalted in Capricorn. This chart looks to me like boiling water. It is a bit tricky asking me this question because I want to see the elements. So I might use an antidote of earth to try to neutralize and sop up the water. We certainly do not want fire because that would create boiling. And Mars is already boiling the water by being in a water a sign. Air would be useless because very emotional people don't understand air. It is like telling a person who is having a tantrum to "go read a book." I would probably use Saturn. Jupiter would increase the conflagration here. Cooling the water down would be appropriate, but the question is how to do that. Should we use a pearl or a moonstone? Should we use Saturn or an earthy remedy? It would really depend how this was presenting.

An example. If this was presenting as one huge case of diarrhea, we would need an astringent which is under Saturn. I say this because Scorpio rules the colon and not every reader would be aware of this fact. This person would be throwing off toxins rapidly, and would probably have bad breathe and acne.

Of all the planets, Mars detests and rebels again suppression, so we would need an activity in order to channel that Mars/Pluto/Uranus in an uniquely Scorpio way like wrestling. I would probably have the client take up wrestling. If the entire chart were to be very scientific in nature, I would suggest a research project or some kind of analysis. This position upon the Ascendant is good for rolfers and welders. I knew a lady welder with a chart like that. Mars rising in Scorpio. I also knew a man who did interrogation for the army. Both of them had Mars rising in Scorpio.

What is the best thing that has happened in your life that has remediated you?

There are several. But the best thing was the rediscovery of the renaissance method of strengthening the heart by wearing certain substances over the heart itself. Dave Roell's amazing publication of Blagrave's *Physic* elucidates this methodology in detail, which I gleefully share.

How do you think the transiting energies come into the energy field of the individual?

There are many theories for this. I believe we are born with receptors to the planets, but in different zones according to one's chart. One theory is such that if you have Mars in Pisces, this then means that you have you have Mars receptors in your feet. If you have Mars in Taurus then you receive your Mars energy in the throat. I personally feel that this occurs through something called "vibrational resonance." We are all made out of vibration and we are all part of the universe. Scientists have discovered that distance is no barrier between two entangled (i.e. bonded) atoms. Once bonded, then two atoms separated by ANY distance, even a million miles will still vibrate together. With this new scientific knowledge, we have a seed for a new theory about how astrological influences work. The scientists call this the "entanglement theory."

So vibration can work through subtle astral light, as light is vibration. If we looked at this in a causative way, we could say that the golden light emitted by transiting Jupiter reaches us, and in some charts and in some signs, this could become pathological. This would be sort of like if I constantly were to point a sound or tone at you and it started to irritate you. This is how the planets can start causing problems.

You can witness this yourself by observing the transits over your own chart. Just wait until Mars conjuncts your Moon by transit. You will most likely notice your Moon getting heated up and you might get a fever or become quite cantankerous. Mars over the Moon will incite the emotions. We know that this works, we just don't really know how.

Physicist Buryl Payne, PhD theorized that water molecules (which are a large part of the air we breathe) have something to do with the transference of astrological influences. I can't remember his exact theory, but it was quite well developed and he did in fact write a paper on the subject. What we do know from the ancients is that each planet and sign has a distinct vibrational quality and influence. We are whirling about in a veritable stew of ever-changing vibrational music. Some vibrations are disharmonious, whereas others are harmonious for our health.

Astrological knowledge allows us some capability to work with these energies. However, astrology is still in a primitive state. Someday when the climate towards astrology becomes positive, this science will become extremely refined. It amazes me that doctors still do routine surgeries without even checking whether or not it is the time of an eclipse! In so doing, we ignore the very best wisdom of our forefathers. In an article entitled *Astrology Heredity*, that was published by Borderlands Research Journal in 1996, I elucidate a number of these concepts in detail.

If this kind of research could be funded, we could be tracking the precise effects of transits over people's charts. Medically.

Explain to the readers in detail how you would go about creating the miraculous curing of a gangrenous foot.

A gangrenous foot would be treated in the manner of the great herbalists. You would take a vat of very hot water and a vat of very cold water, and put the foot from one to the other for many hours, along with the right herbs. Then you would wrap the foot up with the "drawing herbs" and heat. Banana peel or Marshmallow leaves would work. You would then keep changing the leaves, which would pull the putrid matter out of the leg. I've heard three accounts of these methods saving legs that were far gone.

Tell me about your upcoming book on "Remedial Measures and Eclipses."

I've just completed one of the most thorough books on eclipses available, which includes a remedials section on how to offset the potential disturbance of various types of eclipses. It should be out within a year. It includes the effects of each eclipse through all twelve signs. There will be 144 blurbs about each possible combination of sign and house position for eclipses.

How would you attempt to remediate an ankle joint that had deteriorated, inasmuch as the bones were touching together?

That situation is very tough because the cartilage is already gone. So you would probably find a physician who worked with methods of cartilage re-growth and use Glucosamine and Condrointon. They have new methods now that I have seen on TV. They are working with dogs to replace cartilage.

But astrologically you would look at the chart and try to find out how you would enhance the energy of the Moon and Venus and Jupiter, the soft cushioning planets, to assist the physician for more rapid cartilage re-growth if it was possible. Someday, they will be able to squirt something in there and then viola, a person can have new cartilage. I am fascinated with the astrological charts of people who break down cartilage quickly. And I am curious as to what planets rule cartilage, because Saturn rules the hard bones and cartilage protects the bones from each other. It is spongy. It is probably ruled by Jupiter or the Moon, but there is no precedence in astrological literature. I have noticed that people who have broken down cartilage frequently have Jupiter and Saturn misaligned, but I am no expert on this. I am contending with traditional rulership here. I don't see how both the bones and the cartilage could both be ruled by Saturn, as they are so opposite. They are functional opposites. It is a condition that can in some ways only be remediated through a miracle.

Do you have any thoughts on Ethics and Remediation?

If a person doesn't believe in remediation, it won't work usually. Not in every case. Certain religious belief systems can't use certain remedials. For instance, Christian people might feel that it is evil to use some Hindu remedials, or some chants to the planets, so we wouldn't go there. You have to work within the person's religious upbringing and current spiritual values to find a remediation that will work. This is why I make it my business to study different theologies. I study all religions and understand their remedial systems. For instance, the Jewish and Muslim people can respond well to written holy words, these being traditions within their remedial systems that are kosher with their theological view. A Native American individual is content with animal totems. Native American people who have grown up within a Native American spiritual tradition also welcome the assistance of plant spirits. The subconscious of the client must be taken into account.

In reference to the topic of ethics and remediation, the main credo would be:

Do not tread where not welcome.

Another ethical problem is:

Should you alert a family member or friend of an impending aspect and/or what they can do about the aspect they are currently experiencing if it is unrequested of you, and they know you have the ability to do such a thing? My experience is that if they already know you can do that and they do not ask for your help, then your kind advice will be ignored or derided. Remember, no good deed goes unpunished, but there are cases where someone will be grateful. If you see that someone is about to fall off of a cliff, it is your duty to warn them. But again, each situation must be handled uniquely.

Also there is the question as to whether or not you should read charts of a person requesting you to do so. Their children for instance. Yes. The handsome man they met? Not without his permission. I request permission in writing to look at the charts of individual adults who my clients are dating. I view it just as if we are doctors in that we should take our craft seriously and uphold normal privacy ethics.

About Judith Hill

Judith Hill is a life time, second generational astrologer and award winning author. She has performed over 9000 in depth personal readings and is proficient in most branches of Classical Western Astrology including: Vocation, Location, Medical, Natal, Transit-Progressed, Spiritual, Comparative Analysis, Electional (selecting dates for important life events), Gem Selection, Fertility, Dating, and Horary Astrology (the art of answering special questions from exact times). Her consulting experience is vast, having read for men and women of most nations, ages, and professions. She is also well versed in the outside subjects of: Herbology, Vedic Astrology, History, Theology, Illustration arts, Sculpture, Music, Metaphysics, Feng Shui, Phrenology, Physiognomy, Psychology, Palmistry, Graphology and Anthropology.

Judith has served as the "Educational Director" for the San Francisco *National Council for Geocosmic Research (NCGR)* and as a faculty member for *The Institute of Stellar Influence Studies*. She also founded Stellium Press, a publishing house dedicated to fine astrological, whimsical, and spiritual books. Judith has made significant contributions to the scientific and statistical research of Astrology. She has completed reports in both astro-genetics and astro-seismology. Her findings have been included in numerous journals such as: *Borderland Sciences Research Foundation Journal; NCGR Journal; Correlations (UK); The Mountain Astrologer; Dell Horoscope; Above and Below; Linguace Astrale*, and others.

MEDICAL ASTROLOGY 101 Now available!

MODULE 1: The Sun: Vital Force and Life Battery   www.judithhillastrology.com

MODULE 2: The Moon, Distributor of Vital Force

MODULE 3: Mars and Saturn: Cold and Heat, The Source of Dis-ease

MODULE 4: Venus and Jupiter: The "Benefics" or "Good Guys"

MODULE 5: Mercury and Uranus: Electricity, and the Nerves

MODULE 6: Neptune and Pluto: Strange Influences

MODULE 7: The Lunar Nodes: Entry and Exit Portals of Cosmic Energy

MODULE 8: The Four Elements and Three Modes in Traditional Medical Astrology

MODULE 9: Excesses and Deficiencies of the Four Elements

MODULE 10: Let's Read Charts!

MODULE 11: Antidotes for Planetary Pathologies in the Birth Map

MODULE 12: The Transits of Health   www.judithhillastrology.com

AN AUDIO SHOP FOR FASCINATING LECTURES!

THE ASTROLOGY OF MENTAL ILLNESS/ANCIENT LUNAR TIPS FOR THE 21ST CENTURY/SPIRITUAL ASTROLOGY/ECLIPSES/LUNAR NODES IN CHART INTERPRETATION/ MEDICAL ASTROLOGY: CHART SIGNATURES/ SPIRITUAL LESSONS IN THE BIRTH MAP/MEDICAL ASTROLOGY SURVEY/ THE ART OF ASTROLOGICAL TIMING/ ASTRO-PHYSIOGNOMY: PHYSICAL APPEARANCE IN THE BIRTH MAP/UNDERSTANDING MERCURY/ THE ASTROLOGY OF DEATH/THE LUNAR NODES AND SPIRITUAL EVOLUTION/ CHART INTERPRETATION SKILLS/ VOCATIONAL ASTROLOGY: INTRODUCTION/ ASTRO-GENETICS/ THE ASTROLOGY OF EARTHQUAKES/ TRADITIONAL JYOTISH GEM PRESCRIPTIONS FOR PLANETARY WEAKNESSES

STELLIUM PRESS BOOKS: "MEDICAL ASTROLOGY:GUIDE TO PLANETARY PATHOLOGY"/ "VOCATIONAL ASTROLOGY" / "THE LUNAR NODES:YOUR KEY TO EXCELLENT CHART INTERPRETATION" / "THE ASTROLOGICAL BODY TYPES" / "THE PART OF FORTUNE IN ASTROLOGY" / "ASTRO-SEISMOLOGY" / "THE MARS-REDHEAD FILES" / "MRS WINKLER'S CURE"

www.judithhillastrology.com

20

Babies & Children:
Considerations

> Dear Andy,
> I'm still trying to decide what I'm going to write about. But I will answer your questions when I write my story.
>
> P.S. next time I see you can you give me a astrology lessan?

[33]

---

[33] Letter from the notorious philosopher:

                X, age 9.

Remedial Uses of Astrology for Babies

1. Examining the chart to see what might be causing colic, and also what might remedy the problem, depending upon where the stress is coming from.

2. Timing the ending of long days of crying so that parents can pace themselves and get support.

3. Timing the breaking of fevers, the ending of illness, and the magnitude of vibrational stress that is upon a sick baby, in order to make an informed decision about the use of health care.

4. Using a bit of foreknowledge as to when babies will have sleepy times, growth spurts, the need for differentiation, new stimuli, etc.

5. Understanding the vibrational relationship between mothers and fathers and each of their babies.

6. Assisting in finding a nanny who vibes well with a baby, as vibes are of utmost importance at this age. This would be done by checking the composite charts and synastry.

7. Assisting in picking foods that a child might like, depending upon the sign and position of the Moon. Moreover, the baby's chart can indicate time periods in which the baby will be open to new foods. The chart will also show times during which the baby will not feel like eating much, such as when Saturn is upon the Moon.

8. Deciding upon a color to paint the baby's room in order to foster good sleep habits and a sense of well-being.

9. Showing what activities a baby might enjoy. For example a visit to "trampoline city" for a very martian baby, as opposed to a trip to a musical performance for a baby with Venus in Libra upon the Ascendant.

10. Making transitions within time periods that are emotionally positive for the child, such as finding a time during which weaning the baby will be most pleasant and least traumatic for both mother and baby.

11. Consulting the chart as to the best time to encourage a baby to sleep in its own bed, after a period of co-sleeping with the parents (Uranus energies are good for this, as the baby will have a need for freedom and revolution).

12. Consulting the chart as to hairy times for the child's health, so that a working mother could plan to stay home on those days (or have back-up childcare).

13. Watching transits to the child's chart from a young age in order to observe health problems and long term illnesses, such as asthma and food allergies.

14. Knowing from the specifics of the chart what kind of music and arts might best soothe or bring joy to the baby.

15. Analyzing the baby's chart in relation to future step-parents, before merging has begun. This is very important!

Babies

Sun activities for babies: Being recognized and looked at, being cooed at, playing peek-a-boo, going outside to be seen or sit in the Sun, being dressed and getting the hair combed, being talked about, being called a boy or a girl, being identified as an "athlete" or a "princess," actions of discovering the self, looking at the hands and fingers, touching the feet, being bathed.

Moon activities for babies: Snugging, being fed, being told "I love you," sucking on things such as pacifiers, holding a teddy bear or other stuffed animal, crying, smiling, grimacing, saying "mama" or "dada," clinging onto family members.

Mercury activities for babies: Talking, cooing, being talked to, being read to, pointing to objects (this is one of the first markers of language), talking, babbling, listening, interacting, listening to conversations, riding public transportation, being pushed in the stroller, going to the store.

Venus activities for babies: Being kissed, kissing others, drinking mama's milk or juice, smiling, laughing, looking at pretty things and touching them, petting animals, playing, being held by people other than the family, being dressed up in cute outfits, getting the hair combed, listening to music.

Mars activities for babies: Bouncing, moving around, tasting things (this is an active experience for a young baby), poking, tickling, roughhousing, crying, and screaming.

Jupiter activities for babies: Being held by new people, drinking a lot of milk, eating new foods, crawling around the room, getting excited and happy, rubbing food all over the face, having play dates, going on walks, going shopping, going to baby classes, going to the library for a puppet show.

Saturn activities for babies: Swaddling, being worn in a wrap, being put in a confined area such as a crib, playpen, or shut-in area, being constricted by the physical body and trying to master the ability to move within the body, being apart from the mother (if there is also Uranus involved for instance), overcoming limitations.

Neptune activities for babies: Snuggling, bathing, flower essences, homeopathy, breast feeding, soft and soothing music such as Enya or classical music, watching movies, attachment parenting, napping, dreaming, seeing things that adults don't see, talking to entities in the room while laying in the crib.

Uranus activities for babies: Showing the baby a new skill (learning how to smile or take a bite will revolutionize a baby's whole world), letting the baby roll around on a big open floor, taking the baby to a place in which there are new sounds and sights, introducing new colors and objects to the baby, listening to upbeat music or funny and inventive songs.

Pluto activities for babies: Building things around the baby, exposing the child to music and art that matches the intensity of the emotions within in the child, showing the baby the compost pile, worms, spiders, etc.

Lego art by a three-year-old girl with a

Mercury sq. Uranus

Birthday Cake

Mercury square Uranus =
an inventor's mind

Reading the Charts of Children

Avoid-Bad Futuring: When reading the charts of children and babies, it is crucial to avoid the accidental use of words that might label the child as deficient or disordered. If we were to observe a very hard aspect in the baby's chart, it might be very easy to use diagnosing or labeling words for the energies.

Suppose a child arrived in our office with a natal Mercury/Mars conjunction, square to Uranus. We might be tempted to label the personality as hyperactive, schizophrenic, mentally disordered, etc. Instead, it will be more useful to use descriptions of the energies that the soul is needing to express, so that parents can find appropriate receivers for the needs of the child.

We may instead want to say, "This soul will crave a high energy outlet for communication that is exciting and energizing. The mind of this child will have great amounts of energy in regards to subjects and things that will surprise those around her, and the topics of communication at times might be highly innovative."

If the aspect is already exhibiting bizarre symptomology, we will want to also provide a list of outlets for the parents to meet the interesting needs of their child. Perhaps we could encourage this child to make her own radio show, as she will be highly energized to talk during transits to this square. This vibrational mixing could also be expressed through making movies, singing, being an auctioneer, telling intricate stories, or drawing pictures.

Children

1. Timing changes in appetite, and planning for times when children will be open to new food experiences.

2. Checking composite charts with friends in order to ensure that the child is able to thrive within their social sphere.

3. Understanding activities that will come naturally to the child, so that he or she can be begin classes or lessons.

4. Understanding the child's need for discipline and boundaries, as well as the need for differentiation and excitement, so that these needs can somehow be balanced.

5. Understanding weak parts of the child's body in regards to illness and how these tendencies appear in the chart, so that the parent can be prepared with remedial measures before an illness becomes too stressful.

6. Understanding needs that a child can not yet articulate, so that the parent might be more understanding of the nature of what the child is experiencing.

7. Understanding struggles with parents or caretakers. (Is it in the child's natal chart or the composite chart between the parent and child or both? How can the child be respected throughout and within the struggle?)

8. Understanding the child's natural gifts and struggles, so that the parent can help to overcome weaknesses, and maximize talents.

9. Analyzing the chart in order to help parents decide upon a method of schooling for the child; one that will provide the best learning environment for the child's Mercury.

10. Analyzing the chart to see whether or not a child is ready for certain responsibilities, such as owning a pet or having an email account (certain charts are more prone to being responsible than others).

11. Analyzing the chart to see what kind of sporting activities might best suit the child.

12. Noticing what style of dress would be most conducive to expressing the soul of the child in a way that honors their individual character, and the parent's need for decency and order.

13. Examining the chart to see what the child might want to know in regards to adult matters, such as the use and handling of money, food preparation, or trip planning. Every kid has a Saturn, and within certain contexts, he or she will thrive on being schooled in the ways of the world.

Planetary activities for Children

Presentations of Mercury energy in children: Nonstop talking, asking one million questions, not being able to stop interrupting, the compulsive need to vocalize. A blocked Mercury might also present through an inability to articulate words or be understood by others, or being communicatively blocked.

Mercury Redirections: Learning how to read or write, learning new concepts, watching videos that help with language acquisitions such as *Signing Times* or *How to Read by Sounding Out the Letters*. Calling the grandparents, writing one's name, developing one's signature, going on a reading walk (during which you read signs and other words around the neighborhood), writing one's own narrative or the story of one's own life, writing about the family, storytelling, reading books, name games, word games, brainstorming, learning about concepts that relate to writing such as self-expression, learning a second language, singing the alphabet, learning about communicative intent, structure, and rhetoric.

* * *

Presentations of Venus energy in children: Wanting candy or sweets, wanting to see people or not say goodbye, wanting to kiss and be sweet, wanting to dress up and look beautiful, wanting to wear jewelry and make up, wanting to have friends over and have play dates, wanting to buy things, begging for more time to play, offering to give things away, wanting to pick flowers, eat treats, and have snacks.

Venus Redirections: Art projects, making jewelry, playing music, coloring (not focused on following the directions or staying in the lines), dressing up, wearing nail polish, wearing a tie, getting new shoes, going ice skating, eating ice cream, going to a show, seeing a movie, getting a piece of zucchini bread at the local coffee shop, calling a friend on the phone, sending a sweet picture in the mail, arranging flowers, making a collage, playing with stickers, singing together, activities that build camaraderie, making jokes, winking, laughing, hugging, giving compliments, making presents, having a party or celebration.

* * *

Presentations of Mars energy in children: Biting, name-calling, hysterical crying, the inability to sit still, hot face, red cheeks, the inability to follow rules, anger, hostility, tantrums, fits, saying "no," pushing, hitting, frustration, disruptive behaviors, being mean.

Mars Redirections: Roughhousing, playing outside, going to the park, riding a bike, hiking, going on expeditions, intense stroller rides, playing sports, taking off layers in order to cool off, boat rides, eating popsicles and other cooling foods.

* * *

Presentations of Saturn energy in children: Struggles over rules or boundaries, boundary or rule "pushing," refusal to accept rules, crying about the painfulness of life in general, sadness over separation, feelings of oppression, tests of patience, feeling lonely or sad, feeling introverted or inward, not wanting to be around others, having high expectations of the self, playing police, worrying about germs, feeling labeled, feeling confined, feeling different, worrying people don't like them, feeling ashamed, feeling punished, worry, fear of not knowing how to handle new levels of perceptive awareness, an internal need to conquer the surroundings, worrying about future confinement, feeling limited by not being able to eat certain things, behaviors that lead to undesired consequences.

Saturn Redirections: Asking the child to set expectations for himself, allowing the experience of natural consequences, giving the child a specific role, allowing the child to define her own role, separation from the group or time to play alone, projects that include the use of parameters or certain requirements, practicing tactile skills, balancing, jumping, building, teaching skills for negotiating with authority figures, setting clear intentions, allowing children to set their own guidelines and goals, teaching them the art of mitigating between two good choices, quantitative time studies, calendar-making, clock-making, having discussions about conflict-resolution, activities that require problem-solving skills, allowing kids to design their own projects and puzzles, quantitative activities in general, science projects which involve counting and measuring, practicing scales on an instrument, coloring in the lines, guiding the child into the process of creating structure within the self, asking questions such as:

> *What is your approach to brushing your teeth?*
> *What is your artistic vision?*
> *What is your role for clean up time today?*
> *Have you thought about the next hobby you want to take up?*

Presentations of Neptune energy in children: Sleepiness, sluggishness, wanting to snuggle or cling to the parent, oversensitivity to the emotions of others, daydreaming, sleepwalking, nightmares, rashy problems, fears, apprehension, struggles over what is "real" and what is not, confusion, oversensitivity to the needs of others, sorrow over the world's problems, high levels of acuity to fluorescent lights.

Neptune Redirections: Imagination play, coloring, singing, dancing, sleeping, watching movies, reading fairy tales, wearing cozy slippers to school, dressing up, taking photographs, painting, swimming or bathing, making up stories, talking about angels that protect the child, teaching the child about grace and divinity, teaching the child about the spirit within every single sentient being, developing thought forms and pictures in the child's mind that are sweet and loving, teaching children how to control their dreams and how to clear their energy field, relaxation, talking about the night sky, bringing the child to spiritual places, praying for the child, wearing a cross, sending only good thoughts to the child, speaking to the highest version of the child's soul, snuggling, creating a sound that instantly soothes the child, the use of finesse and gentle love, listening to music that is sweet and uplifting.

* * *

Presentations Uranus energy in children: Boredom, the inability to do the same thing anymore or play with the same toys, the need for variety and change, the inability to sit still, feeling antsy, the desire to look at gadgets or technological devices, the inability to contain the self, laughing attacks, the inability to follow rules that the child has been following for some time, rebellion, electricity, eccentricity, bounciness, shaking, or twitching.

Uranus Redirections: Exposing the child to something new, surprising or shocking the child in some way, teaching the child some new skill that will revolutionize the mind, allowing the child a new privilege, taking the child to do something very exciting, teaching the child about electricity, using the element of surprise in daily activities.

* * *

Presentations of Pluto energy in children: Fixation or obsession, clinginess, unwillingness to bend or flex from the object or idea of obsession, power struggles, exuding unbendable power or force, inability of the parent to redirect the child.

Pluto Redirections: Intense energetic and physical experiences, helping the child overcome limitations so they can evolve, healthy obsessions, fixative art projects and creative expressions, bending or pushing clay, moving mounds of soil, remodeling projects, cleaning out the garage, learning about underground systems, composting lessons, any activity where the child can experience a substance or being transform into something else entirely.

21

The Supreme Art of creating
Win-Win Situations:

$$A + B = \text{🌙}\,^{34}$$

---

[34] Otherwise known as the:

Avoidance of Contra-indications

In any case where there exists an extremely hard aspect in the natal chart, there will be a need for a vast array of remedial measures. This is also true of challenging composite charts of individuals who wish to remain together. The reason for this, is that there can be *contra-indications* to certain remedies.

Suppose Mary is a beautiful office manager at a fancy art school, who was born with Neptune in Scorpio upon the Ascendant. Suppose then that the scent of rose oil helps Mary keep her sensitive, neptunian aura clean of other people's vibrations. Now imagine that a new office mate moves in who is allergic to the scent of roses. This would create an official contra-indication. The remedial measure of using rose oil is no longer a viable option.

We must then move to a different sort of scent, or even to an entirely different kind of remedy. Mary might want to try an herb or a homeopathic remedy, which would work internally to somehow remediate the energies. Maybe Mary finds that eating three sauerkraut juice and jelly-soaked raisins for lunch everyday clears her field. This would create an amiable work environment, as the remedial would work towards a win-win situation. Contra-indications can be avoided between siblings, best friends, lovers, co-workers, family members, etc. In close relationships it is important to be persistent and creative until the proper win-win remedial measure is found.

22

The Subtle Art of Glorifying
Stressful Configurations

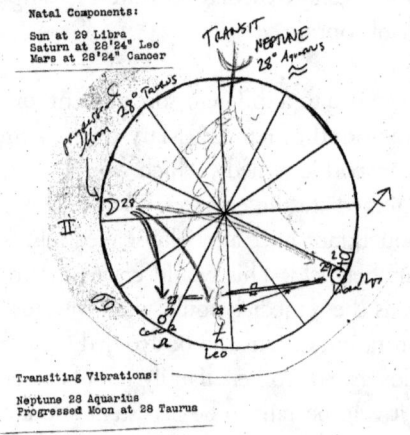

[35]

---

[35] This transiting aspect was channeled into an epic classical/metal saga on the piano entitled *Symphonia Celestalia*.

In the lives of certain individuals, there are highly challenging natal configurations. Some aspect-clusters are extremely hard to handle. In cases that are particularly hard, we may want to employ a variety of methods at once. We might want to look into the possible physical and biological expressions of the energies to see if we can balance the system through dietary changes or herbs. We will also want to channel some of the challenging vibrations into energetic outlets. This is of course a practice in symbolic substitution. One of the most effective remedies for an extremely hard aspect is to give language to the aspect-cluster and do a bit of astral timing around the energy. If we can teach ourselves to recognize a harsh energy within ourselves, we can then inform those around us about how to best help us traverse the aspect gracefully.

On a long term level, we want to make sure to not composite into the same hard aspects that exists in our natal charts. We will want to foster relationships that improve and build upon our tendencies. Moreover, we can plan strategically around the hard energies, allowing ourselves time alone under Saturn, the opportunity to be physical under Mars, etc. The methods through which to nurture particularly hard aspects are infinite. While we have explored a variety of methods through which to remedy such configurations, we must simultaneously accept the fact that certain vibrations seem to be unrelenting. In these cases, we may want to take a palliative care approach.

Palliative care is a specialized form of medical care meant for persons who are enduring a serious illness or time of suffering. The focus of a palliative care approach is to provide relief from the harshness of certain symptoms, pain, and stress. The goal of palliative care is not so much to "cure" a person, but instead to provide pain and stress relief, emotional support, and a good dose of TLC. As astrologers, we might use or recommend certain types of palliative care for fates that seem particularly fated, such as in the case of the following configurations:

> Pluto conjunct the Sun, Pluto square Mars
> Mars conjunct the Sun, Mars square Mars
> Saturn opposing the Sun, Saturn square Mars

In cases as this, an astrologer might cringe and weep when looking at such terrifying aspects. This is also however the point at which an astrologer may want to provide some healing and inspiration through the use of a palliative care approach. The nice thing about palliative care is that it can be used in conjunction with other remedial techniques. For the remainder of this chapter, I will share just a few ideas for dealing with exceedingly hard configurations. May these ideas inspire remedialists everywhere to try to heal the hardest aspects!

Stressful Configurations

Sun/Pluto conjunction in Virgo: This particular person would become severely obsessed with and fixated on tiny little things. Virgo is very focused on details, and Pluto in Virgo can be highly fixated. When she would go out to eat, she couldn't even sit next to a table at which someone was chewing. Yes chewing. At a restaurant. One time, for a school art project in her sound class, she won the "most annoying sound" contest by chewing into the microphone for five minutes straight. She was seriously averse to chewing sounds and various other normal everyday phenomena. She was also extremely clean cut in a very Virgo way. I also watched this person naturally channel the fixative energies into a number of activities, which could even be thought of as natural symbolic substitutions.

Some fruitful uses of a fixated and obsessive tendency:

- Making pointillist drawings
- Painting hundreds of guitar pedals
- Excessive picking and poking and self-grooming
- Working as a dental hygienist
- Editing photographs
- Intense health-focused sports such as cycling

The key to providing Pluto with a remedy seems to be providing an outlet for fixation. Pluto is not a light-hearted and easy-going planet. If a child were to have this aspect, we might suggest very particular and intense activities that involve ordering, sorting, and designing things. The exact suggestions would depend on the layout of the whole chart, and the exact energies and vibrations that were coming into play.

* * *

Mars and Saturn: The energetic combination of these two planets is very effective for accomplishing great amounts of work, but can feel internally frustrating and cause chronic inflammation to the part of the body that correlates to the signs in which the planets are sitting. It can also cause broken bones and other kinds of physical restrictions. Mars/Saturn people seem to be built to accomplish grueling tasks. It is as if they are meant to focus their energies into productive action. Pacing is very important with a Mars/Saturn aspect, as the expectations will be great. No matter what the Mars/Saturn individual takes upon himself, he will want to do it well. If the work is never ending, pacing is the best way to maintain balance and grace.

Sexually this aspect can be very frustrating, as the individual can at times feel blocked from truly being able to relax. I have seen this manifest in various ways through the stories of my clients. Sometimes problems with yeast infections, impotence, or other ailments can make it hard to get the needs met. The phenomenon occurring is that the vibrational field is wanting to open and close at the same time. It is as if the person is starting and stopping simultaneously. It seems that contrived constraint can be very comforting for these individuals, or being dominated by someone who knows what they are doing. A person with high internal expectations can find joy and relief in someone else acting as the Saturn person, by restraining and confining them.

Because a Mars/Saturn connection is a meeting of malefics, it can be challenging to find an apt remedy. This aspect is one of the most challenging, as the person experiences both malefic energies at one time, which usually feels awful inside. These individuals have a desire to do great works, but are often constricted by the confines of the institutions around them. The Mars/Saturn individual can often feel immense pressure with unending expectations. The need for self-sufficiency is crucial, as the internal feeling of being blocked from the desires can constrict the movement a great deal.

During transits to the natal Mars/Saturn, the physical body may begin to hold hot and constrictive energies inside because of an internal feeling of being oppressed. This stress can often be attributed to some sort of external constraint such as money, a job, a project, or an abusive authority figure. The extreme stress of certain Mars/Saturn moments can cause the challenging energies of Mars and Saturn to nestle in the body and show up as chronic inflammatory problems that are often of a rheumatic nature. This could present as asthma, arthritis, TMJ pain, chronic muscle tightness, boils, etc. The nature of the pain depends on the signs involved, but the emotional energy will have a similar hot, cyclical, and locked up feeling. The emotions felt quite often are as follows:

- Frustration, stress, and pressure
- Blockage from getting one's true karmic work done
- Unreasonably high level of self-expectation

Because in certain ways, these could be said to be some of the most challenging energetic combinations, we can learn a great deal by trying to remedy the mixing of Mars and Saturn. Within the pages that follow, I present a few ideas about how to manage a connection between these two planets. The Mars/Saturn remedies listed here can in fact be used during any transit from Mars to Saturn, or conversely, during a Saturn transit to Mars.

These suggestions might also be implemented as "ways of life" for individuals who have the aspect in their natal chart.

Mars/Saturn Remedial Ideas:

1. Soothing music that is also a bit angry or dark, such as Placebo, VNV Nation, and other bands of the morbid/beautiful variety.

2. Hard and tedious work. This work must fall under the value structure of the whole chart. I have seen the following to work beautifully with persons who are successfully filtering these energies through creativity:

- Building a surfboard
- Looking up 2000 words in the dictionary
- Building a metal sculpture
- Tattooing an entire body
- Building a house
- Needlepoint
- Building a business
- Building an intricate wood-worked shed
- Editing one's own photos on photoshop
- Editing film
- Architectural drafting
- Any other tedious yet important work

3. Make sure there is no composite Mars/Saturn connection in future relationships, unless it is somehow mitigated by something extremely loving and awesome, such as a Venus/Jupiter conjunction.

4. Children with a natal Mars/Saturn may do well in the following scenarios:

Listening to dark music without lyrics while drawing intricate pictures that they will then turn into shrinky dinks.

Extremely challenging art projects.

Listening to Chopin while creating structures, such as lining up dominos, building things with legos, pounding a hammer or wrenching on things. Learning and implementing the concept of "practicing" so as to apply this principle to whatever tedious yet highly-productive work or activities they choose.

Note: In certain tough and persistent natal cases, such as in the case of a Sun/Mars/Saturn conjunction, the native may be helped by *structural puncturing*:

Structural puncturing: The act of remediating a blocked up natal Mars/Saturn aspect through hot-energy-extraction techniques. These are techniques that somehow break through the matter-structure of the body (Saturn). Often this is necessary in order to release some of the energy and decrease the physical or emotional pain that is getting locked up in the the physical body.

Examples of structural puncturing: Tattooing, piercing, running a marathon, cutting blackberry bushes, harvesting dangerous sea creatures, climbing a thousand stairs to a temple, jumping up and down 1000 times, self-surgery such as removing slivers and popping zits, hair-plucking, being a soccer or hockey goalie, playing rugby, or any form of self-flagellation, acupuncture, cupping, etc.

Symbolic substitution:

Mars: Puncturing, poking, and cutting.

Saturn: Bones, skin, nails, and structural parts of the body.

The definitions of structural puncturing could be broad, as there are all types of people in the world who prefer to release energy in various kinds of ways. The nature of the exact remediation should fit within the entire scope of the chart, the person's role in life, and the cultural beliefs.

* * *

Mars and Neptune: Mars is hot and Neptune is confusing. When the two come together, it is somewhat like the feeling we get when we have a fever so high that it feels as if we are looking through a fishbowl. At times like this, it can seem that everything is warped because of the heat and how it alters our sensory perception. Mars and Neptune together can also be moist, rashy, yeasty, and fungal. Another interesting expression of Mars and Neptune together is people becoming drunk and belligerent. They can at first be soft and happy and then quickly become randy and cranky. The specific expression of the anger can be seen by the sign and house placement of Mars.

Mars/Neptune Remediations: Combining illusion with physical activity, magic tricks, making films, combining energetic undercurrents with athletics, martial arts, aikido, qi gong, swimming, working out in water, any activity which combines physical activity with spirituality.

Mars and Uranus: The biggest challenge with a Mars/Uranus connection is that it becomes so unexpectedly inflamed. People with this aspect can have a great build up of almost seizure-like flare ups of testosterone, meaning that they will all of a sudden become highly energized. The combined energy of Mars and Uranus together is flurried and chaotic, yet rash and action-oriented. This is the kind of energy that causes accidents. It is hard to protect the body and emotional self when there are bouts of such inflamed chaos. The exact aspect, signs and houses of Mars and Uranus must be considered, and remediations for a Mars/Uranus aspect must be creative and allow the Mars an erratic outlet that is also safe.

Mars/Uranus Remediations: Doing a highly creative and electric project, making a garden that is constantly changing, studying and building robots, baking and decorating creative and inventive cakes, engaging in extreme sports, dressing up in eccentric clothing and going out in public.

* * *

Mars and Pluto: Mars and Pluto together can be quite profound and are only troublesome when the energy becomes overwhelmingly intense. Mars and Pluto can at times be a bit gruesome. The need to express one's sex drive and anger is intense, and there must be a long term remediation that matches the energetic intensity of this vibrational combination.

Mars/Pluto Remediations: Becoming a deep-tissue massage therapist, channeling the energies into intense creative projects and healthy fixations, intense and transformative sex of all varieties, fire based rituals which allow the soul to evolve.

Saturn and Uranus: When this aspect is present, it is crucial to provide activities that allow for innovation and change within structure. We must be very creative in directing a person to activities that allow them to feel ultra free within structure. There are many ways to do this, and the exact nature of the structure/excitement balance depends on the house placements and signs of both Saturn and Uranus, as well as the Ascendant sign and the chart ruler.

The placement of Saturn will show the manner in which the particular soul is seeking to find structure and stability. The placement of Uranus will show where the individual needs excitement, change, innovation, and stimuli.

Saturn/Uranus Remediations: Become a dependable freelancer, work in a different place every day, create an electric structure, become an administrator at an alternative school, create structures that invite and capitalize on the "chaos principle," create a home or business structure that allows for the unexpected.

* * *

Saturn and Neptune: Saturn and Neptune can be very depressing together, as there is a breakdown in the value structure of Saturn. An energetic softening of certain structures can often occur. There are many problem with this aspect, most of them stemming from outside perceptions of what is happening to the native under these influences. Saturn and Neptune together are like driving drunk. Driving is a very saturnian endeavor, as it depends upon the shared reality of not wanting crash. Neptune and Saturn break down the ability to have a shared reality with the world around the individual, in the areas indicated by the chart.

Neptune and Saturn break down trust as well. There can often be a disintegration of shared reality and strong boundaries. Trust is some ways ruled by both Saturn and Neptune, as trust is both an intuitive and behavior-oriented phenomenon; an undercurrent. If people are talking behind one another's backs or whispering, then there will not be trust. Saturn and Neptune create feelings of not trusting authority figures. This is not to say that these are the exact ways that the planets will express themselves, but the presentation would be energetically similar to this feeling in some area of the life.

Saturn/Neptune Remediations: Listening to music while doing work, letting the structures soften a bit, reading old books, using an old typewriter, idealizing authority figures, taking a dance class.

* * *

Saturn and Pluto: Saturn and Pluto together can bring pressure for security, and an intense need for structure, power struggles with authority figures, etc. A good way to remedy this connection is through intense restructuring of the physical form in the areas of the body or life ruled by the placement of Saturn and Pluto. For instance, if Saturn is in the ninth house of the chart, and Pluto hits it, there might be a huge restructuring of the way the individual sees the world, perhaps through the experience of pressure and depravation while traveling, or by not being able to express her ideas in an intense program of some sort.

I have watched the generation of people born with the Saturn/Pluto conjunction in Libra (born between January 1982 and November 1982), intensely try to break down and rebuild relationships, to create emotional and creative security. I remember one client who had this in the third house of remedial education. The Saturn/Pluto generation not only has this conjunction between Saturn and Pluto, but they also have a sextile to this conjunction from Neptune, meaning that there is an element of softness to this generation's intense need to restructure through connection with other individuals. This particular client was involved in a group at school that performed live theater at local community colleges about racism and classism, during which people from the audience became involved in the experience. I witnessed a few of these performances. They were quite intense, and successfully changed people's fixed ideas about race and class. This is an example of a Saturn/Pluto's intense need to break down boundaries and recreate new structures. These individuals are able to restructure entire institutions when they focus on and channel these intense energies.

One of the worst placements of Saturn and Pluto I have seen is a square from Saturn in the twelfth house to Pluto in the third house, in which Saturn was exactly conjunct the South Node. When Pluto hit this square, the native crashed his car twice while driving drunk and almost landed in jail. During his Saturn return, he also cut off his fingers with a saw, which changed the physical shape of his body and bone structure (Saturn), thus affecting his ability to write (third house). Whether the energy of structural death was coming out by crashing cars or changing the bone structure in the part of the body ruled by the placement of Saturn, this energy could be articulated as a "deep intense structural death."

Saturn/Pluto Remediations: Intense structural management, the creation of a new structure, developing a healthy obsession with authority figures and saturnian institutions, transforming a piece of wood into an immaculate sculpture, working on the foundation of a house, tearing down and rebuilding a machine, restructuring the wardrobe to look more professional.

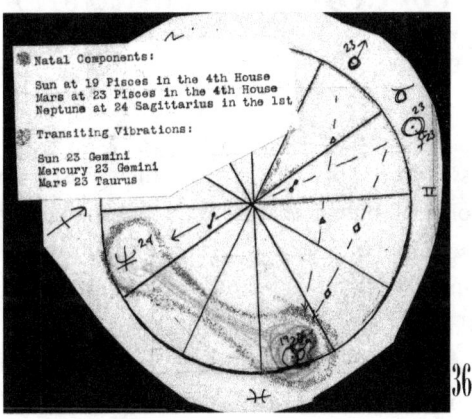

---

[36] A study of a particularly harsh aspect through the use of *Secret Envelopes*. The natal energies of the three planets of *Sun, Mars & Neptune* are configured into a square aspect, creating an intense combination of qualities. When the aspect was ignited by the Sun and Mars, the symptoms presented both physically and emotionally through *inflammatic gushing*.

23

On the Gory Nature of Certain Remediations

As discussed in the previous chapter, there exist a number of aspects or placements that can be quite challenging. An extreme example of a *gory configuration* might be something like a Sun/Mars/Saturn/Uranus conjunction in the twelfth house. This aspect-cluster could easily land a person in jail again and again. There are cases in which the energies of certain charts require various sorts of exciting and sundry remedial measures. In the lives of certain individuals, the underlying energies will be anything but "pretty." It must be noted that certain methods of successful channeling of such energies might also appear *gory* in nature.

In order to maintain the healing non-judgmental lens that astrology inherently provides, we will also want to avoid judging certain forms of remediation. Of course, we never want to suggest anything that would harm a client or someone else, but we do want to keep an open mind. A very simple example of a remedial measure that might be interpreted as *gory* by certain individuals is the use of domination and submission. The act of dominating another person (consensually) can be very healing in certain cases, as can the act of being controlled. A dominant person might be able to help us harness and control ourselves during hairy time periods. This can be likened to wearing earplugs during a loud metal show. Without earplugs, such music and intense vibration can be disharmonious and even disturbing. A consensual listening to such music, combined with a barrier to the eardrums, can turn such music into something that is utterly appealing.

Intense experiences do in fact clear pent up energies. This is perhaps why intense people often end up at loud concerts, fighting and brawling out their rage. While the act of moshing or dominating another person isn't always accepted as an appropriate activity to encourage in our culture, these activities do in fact happen naturally each and every single day. Teachers dominate unruly students, parents dominate toddlers, etc. Certain charts require and thrive on authority figures to either build them up or oppress them. Suppose a person has a natal Mars opposed Saturn. In the early years it could have been true that the child's ability to do work and express aggression were continually squashed by Saturn individuals. In the older years, the Saturn-squelching can become internalized and be projected onto others.

Pluto requires a different kind of experience. The intent of Pluto is not to separate, but to connect and transform on a very deep level. The need for power and control is inherent with Pluto, and thus these themes will almost always come up when there is a plutonian influence. This is the kind of control that is mental in nature, such as the use of jealousy, intense manipulation, etc. Pluto calls for control of a mental and energetic nature. Suppose a certain individual were to have a Pluto/Venus conjunction in the natal chart in the eleventh house in Libra.

At times, a person such as this will intensely befriend new people, get mentally and energetically sucked into their experience, and transform themselves in some way through the process. If the partner has a hard time with this, then the remediation must be as energetically potent as the experience of connection itself. Thus, the partner must "upgrade" the intensity with which she is providing stimulating and attractive energies. Perhaps a Venus/Pluto person requires a bit of "healthy jealousy" in order to stay interested. A healthy jealousy can be one that constantly reminds us of the fact that our partner is interesting, a hot commodity, or attractive to other individuals. This is not necessarily a negative thing. The important point to remember here is that some vibes are rather bizarre. This is what makes life interesting!

As remedialists, we may encounter problems that have already passed through other forms of healing, only to persist. It is of utmost importance that we keep an open mind so that we might be able to invent remedials for even the hairiest of conundrums. This will aid us in maintaining and utilizing astrology's non-judgmental lens in order to relieve suffering.

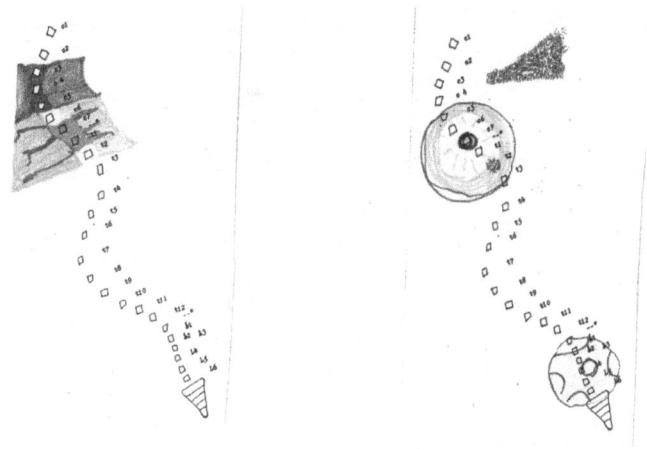

A look into the astral spine may lead to some graceful ideas for moving through intense vibes.

24

On the Remediation of Addiction:

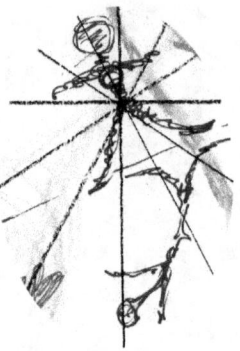

A move towards Balance

As an astrologer, one of my hardest challenges has been dealing with addiction. There are many thoughts on addiction in the modern era. Certain astrological authors suggest that addiction be attributed to Neptune or the twelfth house, while others might discuss addiction as phenomenon related to Pluto. It is in fact true that Pluto brings the energy of fixation, while Neptune can create the feeling of not being able to handle the harshness of life. In both cases, such feelings can in fact create behaviors that we might label *addictions*.

These influences can affect a person's ability to thrive "normally" or in a way that is sustainable on the earth plane. Addiction is something that plagues people in our modern society, in that addictions seem to be understood as anything that brings people down, makes them less happy about themselves, etc., which they have an unwanted compulsion to continue doing. If we think of addictive behaviors as those actions that a person wishes he or she could stop doing but cannot, then this indicates an imbalance in the system.

When trying to help someone who is suffering from an addiction, we can start by attempting to deconstruct what that person has been taught about addiction. Also, because the word "addiction" is an abstract one, we will want to find out exactly what it means in the everyday life. The feeling of being addicted to something is hard to break. In fact, once we have developed a synaptic connection between the concept of happiness and a certain substance or behavior, we have set up a paucity principle. In other words, there now exists the idea that there is not enough of the certain addictive substance. Or in the case of a certain behavior (such as unhealthy eating), the behavior gets labeled as "bad," creating the feeling that one's existence is problematic.

In our culture, we have developed the conversation that certain addictions are a disease, of which a person has no apparent choice. It could in fact be true that addiction is not an incurable illness, but instead a taught framework of mind, with synaptic threads connected between the addictive substance and the concept of joy or contentment. If this were true, then we would know that the suffering of addiction could be handled by making new synaptic connections. Physical touching creates synaptic connections. Touching a face can create a synaptic connection to it. Touching a cigarette throughout the day can also create a synaptic connection.

While it is valid to create synaptic connections with an object or person that best remediates the energies at the time, people can also create synaptic bonds with objects or behaviors that seem to contribute to suffering.

When this kind of situation occurs, it will be most pleasurable for that person to stop connecting with such things or substances that have become tedious to the mental health and well-being. Oftentimes, there is a soul-need that is underlying the addictive behavior. Perhaps a person is needing a great deal of community, and has been meeting this need through a group of smokers. In this case, a feeling of community is created through the common synaptic bonding that occurs when people bum a smoke or pass a joint. Community can in fact be created without substances. What we will want to notice is what planets in the chart are contributing to the imbalance. A person may have more than one addiction, and in these cases, the problem can often be located in two distinct aspect clusters.

Now let us try a fun little mental activity. Find a quiet spot where you will not be distracted. Now try the activity in the footnote below[37].

This little challenge is a tiny glimpse into the art of *accidentally creating a fixation*. This can easily happen when we create a situation where we must think about the visual image of something in order to figure out how to not think about that thing. It seems that this is how many mental habits can be formed around substances. We are told that the thing we are doing is bad or wrong, and then we start thinking about how we are bad to do it, and this makes us want it more.

When balancing out the system after a time of imbalance, it will be quite helpful to focus on the actions and behaviors in which we would like to engage (as opposed to the thing we are trying to stop doing). If we can bring fulfillment to the soul-needs of each planet, it could be said that we will feel whole inside. If we can work towards this feeling, the imbalancing behaviors will fall away in a more natural manner. There will indeed be emotions that accompany the cessation of any emotionally driven activity, and these internal wellings will be stronger on certain transits. Because we will be able to watch the traveling planets, we can be prepared for the entire gamut of the soul's needs. We can have activities and ideas at hand in order to honor each facet of our existence. It will be helpful for each of us to clarify our soul-needs so that we can thrive!

---

[37] For the next 30 seconds, do everything you can to NOT think about:

Ten onions dancing around a pickle.

A Holistic Approach to Rebalancing the System

When we are wanting to re-balance our system after a period of use of a certain substance, it will be important to allow the physical and emotional body to transition as naturally as possible. This is true of any shift involving a new or different approach to handling the physical and emotional needs. That being said, it is important to approach a *systemic re-balancing* according to the quality of time as indicated by the chart. The evolution to new habits can be quick on certain Uranus transits, or be more slow and reconstructive under certain Saturn energies.

Because astrology is linked to the qualitative experience of time, it is helpful to remember that each person will tend to transition in their own manner, which will surely differ depending on the current astral influences. A person who is under the influence of Uranus might find the liberation from alcohol use to be easy and lightening. A person who has Saturn traveling through the sixth house of health and well-being might find success in transitioning off of xanax through a more systematic approach to health and well-being. Either way, it is important to understand that all forms of drugs and alcohol can be thought of as soothing agents. Just like any pill or healing technique, there are times that we do not want to continue with a remedy because the illness has been cured or the physical pain has subsided. When a person who is using a substance to medicate an emotional problem is able to heal on the soul-level and is ready to decrease their use, we can provide ideas to help along the way. We will want to create a healthy list of activities for each planet. If we attend to the whole system, the change will most likely be soothing and successful.

Sun Outlets: Drinking water (especially electrolyte water or distilled water), walking[38], hot baths, showers, saunas, mineral baths, laying in the sun, grooming the body, attending to the wardrobe, designing one's own look.

Moon Outlets: Long baths, keeping extremely good foods in the house at all times, uplifting music or music to help release emotions, employing the use of emotion-based coping skills, hugging, eating comfort foods, singing.

Mercury Outlets: Creating and maintaining balance-oriented language (concepts such as *portion control* or *healthy baseline*), giving the mind something to do, getting really into a new form of media, joining a new group, providing new stimuli to the senses, learning how to sew, learning about every hiking trail in your area.

Venus Outlets: Connecting through sharing the true feelings, making and giving gifts, baking sweet treats, or looking beautiful.

Mars Outlets: Venting, kicking a soccer ball against the house (no windows), walking, doing tedious projects that are filled with love (beading, braiding, etc.), cleaning, being left alone.

Jupiter Outlets: Finding opportunities we want to create for ourselves, planning trips and other ways to let loose, dancing, paying attention to activities that make us feel free from the constraints of life.

---

[38] Walking helps move energy during the depressing or unpleasant times, helping the body speed up any healing process. (*Walking while listening to uplifting music on noise-canceling headphones really does the trick!*)

Saturn Outlets: Crying to clean out toxins, practicing concrete activities (mathematics, counting, editing), employing the use of problem-focused coping (focusing on the concrete steps it takes to fix the conundrum).

Uranus Outlets: Doing something entirely new, shocking oneself, allowing the self to get nervous or embarrassed, changing plans and calling in sick once in a while, merging with new people for short activities and projects, having parties.

Neptune Outlets: Taking up an artistic endeavor, finding a forum to discuss high-minded concepts (the unseen realm, or subtle realities), working with any form of spiritual discipline that focuses on the highest good in all divine beings.

Pluto Outlets: Intense focus on transforming our environment, conquering our surroundings, tearing down walls, taking out windows, building a skate ramp (for a teenager), fixating on something we want that will remind others of the inherent power of being alive.

Balancing Foods for Remedial Transition

Whole grains
Vegetables
Goat and sheep cheese
Homemade pizza
Halloumi
Mineral Water
Eggs, fish, and chicken
Homemade junk food
Avocados
Pure cranberry juice
Live culture yogurt
Homemade sweets
Whole fruits of all kinds
Sesame Oil
Teas of all kinds
Homemade breads
Maple syrup
Raw honey
Miso
Butter
Beans
Nuts
Sauces
Artisanal foods
Fermented foods of all kinds
Kosher foods
Anything made with LOVE

Liver Cleanse: milk thistle extract, dandelion root tea, whole grains garlic, an apple a day, green tea, grapefruits, lemons, limes, walnuts, turmeric[39].

---

[39] The major fat burning organ in your body, the liver cleans the blood stream from medications and toxins, and is the energy-production factory. Gotta take care of that little guy, as the *soul* is said to run throughout our blood. We want clean travels!

Case Study:

Can we remedy addiction through the use of
Secret Envelopes?

> 3) My main addiction, which I have basically struggled with all my adult life, has to deal with body image and food. It has been increasingly bothersome the past couple of years, as I've had to readjust my diet due to food allergies. Combining these factors with a fear of aging, every food choice I make feels like an enormous decision that I either rejoice in, or beat myself up for the rest of the day.[40]

We can ask any or all of the following questions:

> How would you define addiction?
> What substances or things are you addicted to?
> Do all of your addictions feel the same?
> Has another person ever told you that you were addicted to something?
> Can you imagine a visual image of addiction in your mind?
> What does it look like?
> Do you believe in addiction?
> When did you come out as an addict?
> How does the word addiction serve you?
> Is anything more exciting than the addictive substance?

---

[40] I put out a call to "addicts," so that I might learn something about remediating addiction through astrology. I received a response from a young woman whom I had never met. I sent her a letter with some questions in it. This is how she defined her addiction. It will of course be true that each person will understand addiction differently, as the word *addiction* itself is an abstract one.

K.M. responded to my call for "addicts"

We exchanged a few letters, and it turns out that her addiction was connected with food.

The problem in the chart was obvious.

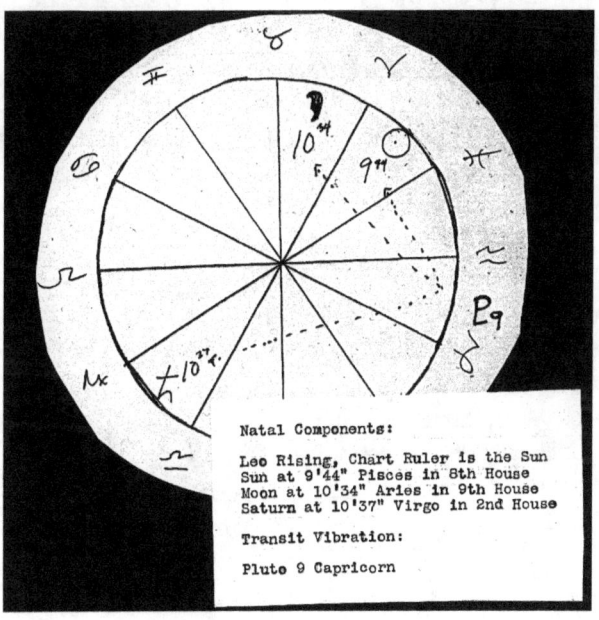

Natal Components:

Leo Rising, Chart Ruler is the Sun
Sun at 9'44" Pisces in 8th House
Moon at 10'34" Aries in 9th House
Saturn at 10'37" Virgo in 2nd House

Transit Vibration:

Pluto 9 Capricorn

Both the planet of her **physical identity** (*the Sun*) & the planet of her **appetites** (*the Moon*) are **constricted** by Saturn in Virgo.

Sun at 9 Pisces = Energetically sensitive and ethereal
Moon at 10 Aries = Ravenous and exciting appetite
Saturn at 10 Virgo = Highly constrictive, critical, harsh, detailed, particular, picky, etc.

> "Ok, 20 possible uses of Saturn in Virgo, not dealing with food.
> 1) Washing the floors with a different essential oil according to the moon cycle or astrological cycles.
> 2) Designing a font with excrutiating detail.
> 3) Illustrating the anatomy of the human body to learn the muscles, etc.
> 4) Learning how to web code.
> 5) Waking + following a tight daily schedule according to the bodys' circadian rhythms (Chinese Med. Organ Clock)
> 6) Rearranging all my very tiny knick-knacks in my cabin.
> 7) Learning a new language.
> 8) Documenting events into charts & infographics.
> 9) Beading highly-detailed jewelry.
> 10) Organizing the files on my computer.
> 11) Learning advanced science + math concepts.
> 12) Saving money by being ultra conservative.
> 13) Collecting + drying seeds from nature.
> 14) Keeping an accurate checking acct. ledger.
> 15) Making bins to organize laundry colors.

We worked together to find a more varied and interesting palette of ways to use the Saturn in Virgo.

25

Food Love:

An Interview with
Yoshihiro Matsuoka

-

Metal Sculptor
Builder
Custom House Artist
Surfer
Neighbor
Chef
Deep Sea Diver
Scorpio

41

---

[41] In this important chapter, we look at food through the lens of a...

Moon/Venus/Jupiter conjunction in Libra

How did you learn to cook?

Mostly started cooking when I started living by myself when I was 19 years old. I would cook whatever I wanted to eat over and over until I was sick of it. I always would want to do something new. You must cook something over and over again to really learn it.

How do you plan your meals?

Usually one ingredient dictates the rest. I go to the store and find something that looks good and then start from there. Sometimes you know what you want to eat and you go from there. Shopping is fun. That's where you generate ideas for cooking. At times, my body will have a craving for something, and I will plan the meal around that. If I don't feel any particular way about it, then I will go to the store and check it out.

If you get sick with a cold, like a runny nose and fever, do you change your diet at all?

Um yeah. Definitely. I guess that making the food depends on the time and the feeling of the day. So you are sick and you don't want to eat something heavy or greasy or spicy. Something simple; soup. That's universal. For asians, it is rice porridge, also called kayu; I guess that's a traditional old school food when you are sick. I remember my grandparents making that and my mom making that for me when I was sick. Really simple, just boiled down rice with Umeboshi. And miso soup. Clear soup. Something light.

Do you eat sweets?

Hardly any.

Do you take medications?

None. Besides alcohol.

If you are feeling rambunctious what do you eat?

You are happy, you kind wanna eat something, "orgasm in your mouth type of thing." A lot of japanese little foods are like that, like sushi or hot food. A bit of spicy food or whatever.

When you were in art school, making a lot of metal sculptures, what did you eat?

In school, I was never making lunch. It's school time, and you are really busy with school and you just go out and get pizza. Garbage is what you are eating. Lots of coffee. Coffee and garbage.

What is "emergency food?"

Spaghetti is a staple thing, more so than Top Ramen, but Top Ramen is easy to cook. So spaghetti and Top Ramen. Both are quicker than cooking rice.

What is the most important thing to have in your kitchen?

As in a material thing? A knife and cutting board. Why? It's where everything starts.

Do you ever force yourself to eat?

Not really.

How do you know when it is time to stop eating?

That's funny. That's when you are ready to drink.

If someone you knew was throwing up, what would you feed them?

Light tea.   Silver tea. Silver tea is hot water with a slice of ginger in it. At least that's what I call it. I wouldn't try to give them any food.   I don't want to eat anything when I am throwing up.

Do you ever worry about your health?

Yeah. Don't we all? You know my mom used to say, "eat thirty different kinds of food, not food but ingredients, each day"...kind of thing. Your body knows you are overdoing it on certain things. Kinda. Variety is very important.

What is the most important thing your mom taught you about cooking?

Watch out for salt. In Japan there is a tendency of over-salting everything, and I think I was using a lot of salt on everything. And the thirty ingredients a day thing. The salt part is most personal, because of the kidney thing. She had a kidney failure later in life. Salt hurts the kidneys. Salt is very, very dangerous. So is sugar. It's about balance.

Do you eat meat, and how often and what kinds?

I love meat, but I don't have to have meat in every meal or every day. And it doesn't have to be in large quantities. I like meat that is complimenting the rest of the meal. A little bit of meat with lots of other stuff.

What is your recipe for Miso soup?

A simple one. Kombu. Soak it in cold water. Bring it to boil. Add katsuobushi, which is bonito flakes. And then make a dashi stock. And then you add miso. With residual heat. Turn the heat off before you add the miso, as you don't want to boil the miso.

Do you think that food holds energy?

Yeah. Definitely. Food is the energy. The fuel.

If you were going to cook dinner for a lady and you wanted to impress her, what would you make?

Ha. I would cook her some aphrodisiac food, like oysters, seafood in general. What do you call it, fun foods. Like exotic foods, interesting foods, definitely. Pickled foods. Fermented foods. Pickles [42].

What are your favorite foods to put in tiny dishes?

Condiments. Like green onions. Sliced super fine. Pickles. Pickled vegetables. Sauces. I guess I'm not really the saucy guy. I don't do sauces much.

If you had ten dollars, what food would you buy?

My friend Rachey just got me a "scratch it" and I won ten bucks. And I love Pho, that vietnamese noodle soup. And nowadays a bowl of Pho is eight bucks plus tip. That's what I would do with it.

---

[42] Brine recipe for pickling & fermenting:

1/4 non-iodized salt: 1 cup water

Fermenting recipe: Pour brine over vegetable to be fermented, leave on the counter until you can smell it and it has been bubbling for a few days. Scrape mold off top and taste it. Ferment to taste, the refrigerate to slow down the process. Eat often and voraciously. *AG*

How do you cook fish?

I would almost say you don't cook it. But trouts I just salt them. No pepper no nothing. Just salt. You put it on a low heat grill. Salt glazed. It's covered in salt. And then that will keep the fish in tact, all in one piece. It protects it from falling apart. The skin will stay together. And then the fish will absorb the salt. It is simple and yummy and it is the best way to cook trout.

Ocean fish, you basically want to eat raw because they are good the as is. Sashimi, that is what I eat. Fatty fish, I would make a soup out of it. Black cod, especially. Makes a really good broth as well.

Breaded fish. I've done it. The result is not worth the effort.

I would cook fish always in half vegetable oil and half butter, NOT olive oil. This actually applies to all meat as well. And sautéing in general.

What is the benefit of pickled vegetables?

They are pikros[43].

---

[43] *Pikros* is an ancient Greek flavor used by Vettius Valens. He attributes the flavor of *pikros* to Mars, and the flavor of *pikros* itself can be described as:

1. *A sharp and pungent taste.*

2. *A food that was expected to be pleasant and is instead unpleasant or bitter.*

Vettius Valens, p 14 (*Translator: Gehrz*)

If someone had intestinal problems, how would you cook for them?

Is the problem digestional or a problem of absorption? Or is the stool loose or tight? I would suggest...well in Japan if you are sick you get porridge and then pickled vegetables. Always umeboshi. That is the king of the pickle. It's known for a miracle cure. It is notorious for curing incurable diseases. You go to Japan, if you are sick, people will traditionally give you rice porridge with umeboshi in it. In certain regions, they might add various kinds of stock to the porridge as well.

How would you go about making a broth?

I assume you are talking about dashi. Dashi is Japanese fish-based stock. It is used for pretty much all Japanese cooking. It is basically made of kelp seaweed, which is also called Kombu, and Katsuobushi, which is bonito flakes. First step is to boil the water with a chunk of Kombu in it. Bring it to a boil, turn the heat off, then take the kombu out, and put the bonito flakes in. Then take the bonito flakes out after one minute. That is it.[44]

---

[44] Dashi Broth

Put some Kelp and a few dried Shitaki mushrooms
in a pot of water.
Bring to boil.
Turn off heat.
Toss in some bonito flakes.
Let sit for a few minutes.
Strain into jar or pot to use for miso soup, sauce, etc.

26

Navigating Transitions

I have noticed a very real phenomenon among both clients and friends. It is a phenomenon that occurs when people have been through a very bad transit, or a slew of hard energies in a short period of time. People can often subconsciously fear that this same bad thing will happen to them again and again, especially if the hard energy was played out in a relationship. A person can begin to think that the transiting energies are "who they are now," or that the rest of their life is doomed to be equally as hard as the period they have just endured.

This is of course mathematically impossible, because new transits and progressions are coming in every single day! There will be almost always be new relationships, friendships, children, or neighbors coming in, which will inherently alter the energetic playing field of life. The astrological chart is a moving portrait. The energies of our natal charts are constantly evolving as our auric field mingles with the vibrations around us. Now let us give language to the stressful condition of fearing the future on account of challenging situations from the past: *Post Traumatic Transit Syndrome*. While there are probably endless variations on PTTS, let us call one version of this phenomenon the *Subconscious Fear Variety*.

Post Traumatic Transit Syndrome
Subconscious Fear Variety:

The subconscious fear that the hard times will last forever.

The subconscious fear that these problems will come back again and again.

The feeling of being forever doomed.

This syndrome could of course be likened to a case of *Post Traumatic Stress Disorder* (PTSD), which can include many various side effects such as anxiety, depression, fear, feelings of hopelessness, etc. Post Traumatic Stress Disorder typically comes after a person has sustained a period of great horror of one type or another, such as being in the army and watching friends die in battle, being in an abusive relationship, or having a horrible work situation for five straight years. The worst part of PTSD seems to occur when people who have experienced extreme things are then expected to "come back to real life" and act like everything is "fine." This seems to worsen the disconnect between how a person feels inside and how they are perceived through the eyes of others.

In astrological terms, Post Traumatic Transit Disorder can be caused by any number of hard or unmanageable transits. Suppose that one person in a couple is under the extreme rays of Pluto, causing each and every one of those person's relationships to change entirely on account of an addiction of some kind. The existing structure of friendships will surely cease to exist in this case, and new ones will begin.

In any case that a person has been through an extremely hard time, it will be quite healing to work with them to transition into a brighter future. This process might include any number of steps, but the first step is commonly to purge the past feelings of angst. An everyday example of this fact can be seen in women who have recently given birth. These woman often have a need to tell their birth story again and again. This seems to be an integral step in purging the intensity of the experience. Through this process of purging an intense experience through storytelling, the experience itself becomes a less potent memory.

One thing we can do with clients who are coming out of a long period of planetary duress is provide a concrete date for the *end of suffering*. During this process, we can also remind the person that certain transits will never occur again in the lifetime (especially in the case of Pluto). Or, if the same transit will in fact occur again (such as in the case of a Saturn return, which happens a second time around the age of 58 or 59), we might say something like this:

You know, you have done a very good job of handling this very hard time period. You aren't going to have to do this exact struggle again for another 29 years, and by that time you will be much older and wiser in general. This means that you will also be better equipped to gracefully handle difficult energies.

Let us look at another form of Post Traumatic Transit Syndrome:

Post Traumatic Transit Syndrome:
Shame Variety

The feelings of shame and embarrassment over certain behaviors and experiences that have accompanied a hard transit or bad composite chart relationship. Also, the subtle belief that one has "become" the shameful behaviors, or that the life is doomed in any other way on account of these passing energies.

As astrologers, we have a great amount of power to heal clients coming out of phases such as this. The inherent nature of the constantly changing planetary positions, allow for healing to occur, in that astrology reminds us that change is inevitable.

People are at times *seized by the planetary rays* as a transit comes into the chart, which impels them to take certain actions. The transits can urge us to want to do things that do not seem in any way logical or normal within the existing context of the life.

In cases such as these, there might exist the need to do a bit of un-shaming. A person may need help either integrating the new urges (if they are here to stay on account of a stationing progression for instance), or in giving positive language to the changes that have occurred on account of being seized by the planets.

It can also be said that many interesting and magical experiences can occur on account of the planetary energies seizing us. We can remind our clients of the simple fact that interesting circumstances make for good stories.

Another method of unshaming is to remind the client of the "larger purposes" that have shown themselves to unfold throughout the course of the intense transit. We could do this in an infinite number of ways, such as recapping the changes of the entire transit, or seeking another astrologer's helpful perspective on the exact transit.

It is also very helpful when leading clients through *transit-transitions,* to help integrate the story of the new vibrations that are entering into the life, with the story of the life thus far. The reality is that astrologers handle a great number of transitions every day as we work with our clients. One thing that can happen, and especially so with certain minds, is that people crave past experiences and the feelings of certain time periods. This leads to a tendency to try to recreate past experiences, which often does not quite work, as the same exact set of energetic and planetary combinations doesn't tend to repeat itself ever! A more uplifting mind frame to encourage is to be excited about the process of continually creating interesting experiences as the planetary energies change and morph throughout life.

As astrologers, we can remind clients that certain situations they are currently experiencing will hint at time periods in the past. At times, we can find it useful to look into the past to talk about how part of the natal chart has morphed throughout time. This would be in the case that the client is dealing with a certain part of the chart very acutely and in a focused manner. An analysis of the past can help integrate the current experiences into a whole understanding of the self.

Example: Let us suppose that a person is born with a natal Saturn in the third house, and that transiting Neptune were coming up to oppose that natal Saturn from the ninth house.

Natal energy: Saturn in the third house.

Transiting influence: Neptune traveling through the ninth house.

Because the natal mind is very structure-oriented on account of Saturn being in the third house, it might be very healing for the client to hear something like this:

I just want you to know that, in the totality of your life, your mind is quite logical; suited to systems and pattern-recognition, such as in languages, mathematics, etc. Right now, however, the normally structured nature of your mind is being softened up a bit; a process which will last until January of 2013. It is also important to remember that, no matter how softened your mind becomes, it will never dissolve its crystallized understanding of things. In other words, this is just a phase. Don't sweat it.

By providing our clients with positive stories about the shifts that are happening to them, we contribute to positive thinking and brighter futures. When making future predictions, we can do so with a graceful heart, knowing that everything we say can and will affect the experience of our client for years to come. When we use future predictions in order to assist a person in transitioning through their energies, we are simultaneously helping that person maintain a healthy and integrated self-identity and feeling of peace about the soul's path.

Another circumstance in which it is important to help with transitions, is a case in which a client has been using a self-remedial such as drinking alcohol, smoking cigarettes, smoking pot, etc., and is ready to transition out of this remedial method. Or in the case that a person is using some other remedial that is no longer helping the initial problem. When a remedial measure has begun to cause other problems, then it is useful to transition to other forms of remediation that will work with the current influx of energies.

While I was interpreting a leadership seminar at a local university, the class read a book called *Managing Transitions*, which focused on transitions within the school system. While the school system has little to do with astrology, the whole discussion got me thinking nonetheless. One of the main points of the book, was the idea that in any transition, there is a period of grieving the loss of the things that we are losing.

After a period of grieving the loss of a substance or behavior, There also exists a liminal space in which any transitioning person feels out of sorts, not knowing what to do with the focus that was once given to the old substance or situation. It is from this confusing and aimless time period that the new self is born, as the soul is given time and space to integrate new remedials and activities of enjoyment into the everyday life.

As I watch my friends and clients attempt to quit smoking cigarettes, cut down on drinking, etc., I often hear the same assumptions as they talk about quitting. The underlying subconscious assumption is often:

If I were a good person, or a strong person, I could just stop using this drug and be fine with it. I am weak. I am going to fail.

But as I learned in the leadership seminar, any change can be looked at as a transition, and transitioning is a process. From astrology, we know that there are various sorts of moods that can accompany any transition. In fact, the manner in which we experience any transition depends quite a bit on the planetary transits we are experiencing at the time. Saturn transitions can feel full of deprivation. Uranus is usually felt as a surprising influence, while Pluto might bring a grief of an obsessive and intense nature. Neptune can often feel confusing. It is important to have a good list of tools and tricks in order to successfully move through all sorts of transits, progressions, composite-mergings, etc.

Moving Clients Through Transitions

1. Witness the past trauma with them.

Explain that you notice that there has been a recent trauma.

Describe explicitly to them what the time period might have felt like physically, emotionally, or mentally.

2. Speak to the highest values of the trauma.

Explain the importance of the experience on account of the highest values of the planets involved.

Ex: *Mars* = Differentiation, passion, incitement.

Saturn = Self-care, grooming. clearing clutter, longing for a better life, structuring, restructuring.

Uranus = Revolution, excitement, freedom to evolve.

Neptune = Dissolution of matter, subtle understanding, unique perceptive capabilities.

Pluto = The experience of soul-alchemy, a deep understanding of controlling the qi.

3. Move through the energies of the trauma.

Do this in whatever manner works best for the exact context of the situation. This will depend on the chart of the client, and our specific strengths as a remedialist. Anything could be expected to work, as long as it encourages pent up fear, sorrow, or hopelessness to be expressed.

Some ideas: Talk with the person as they cry, laugh with them, lighten the heaviness with jokes, sing to them, be very logical about their trauma. Say, "I am so sorry this happened to you," hug them, high five them and say, "You are almost done with a really challenging year!" Read a bible passage to them (if they would find this soothing), tell them a story, rearticulate the experience back to them. Look them straight in the eyes with love in your heart. Ask them questions about the experience, dig deeper; draw the visual, emotional, and mental elements of the experience out of them, if they are willing.

4. Engage in problem-based coping strategies.

Speak to the highest future possibilities of the transitions that are occurring. Refer the client to any services that might help them successfully control or change their environment for the better. Teach them new concepts that will help them as they walk through the transitions at hand.

5. Engage emotion-based coping techniques.

Suggest activities that will be most positive for the Moon sign and the entire chart. Prescribe emotional outlets that will also be good for the physical and mental bodies.

6. Leave the client on a good note.

Provide a hearty list of symbolic substitutions, physical remediations, and a mind full of positive thinking. End the reading with a look into the next few Jupiter and Venus transits and write down time periods during which they can enjoy inspiring, optimistic, and happy vibrations. Remind the client that they are doing good work through their hard experiences, and that they are spiraling upwards through strife.

Case Study: How can we help a person who is going through a major transition? The intense transit of *Uranus **conjuncting** natal Saturn in Pisces in the 7th house.*

Virgo Rising
Natal Saturn in Pisces in the 7th House
Saturn ruling Aquarius on the 6th House
Transiting Uranus conjunct natal Saturn

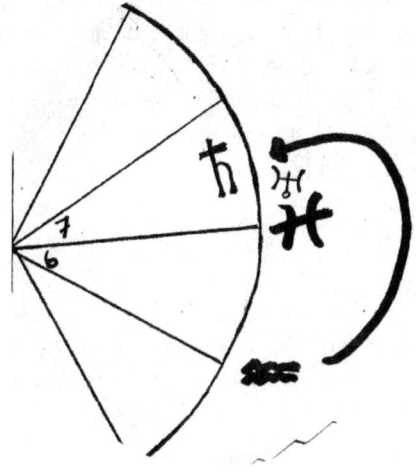

Transiting Uranus rocks natal: ***Saturn in Pisces***

Problematic Presentations:

Unexpected changes in the structure of the foot.
Sudden collapse of work situation on account of the
inability to wait tables any longer.
Inability to walk.
Breakdown of marriage.

Analysis: It will be quite important in this case to guide our client through the intense, de-structuring mayhem of this Uranus conjunct Saturn transit. This can happen through many methods, beginning with a non-judgmental assurance that life will not be chaotic nor upsetting forever. We could also look to some happy times in the future, as well as try to come up with a list of remedial outlets for the intensely uncomfortable energies. The client will most likely also feel healed by the fact that we have witnessed their internal experience, which can bring back a feeling of wholeness. Because the nature of this transit is to be quite jarring, we will also want to release some of the natural fear associated with the transition through whatever methods work best within our remedial tool kit. Timing the end of the struggle will be quite effective, as will locating joyful times in the near future.

Possible Remediations: Preparing for upcoming Saturn/Uranus, experiences by brainstorming new and exciting job opportunities and changes, a focus on changing and innovating the beauty of the footwear as to enliven the possibilities for a new Piscean structure, building one's own pair of shoes to give the hands something to do during the unsettling time, decorating the foot with an exciting anklet or something tied around the toe, a change in the sleep schedule, working at weird and different times, and changing the structure of the life in general.

Extras

Glossary

Aspect: An angle between two planets.

Astral Body: The energy sphere that surrounds and is connected to an individual; also known as the aura, the chakra field, or the energy-body.

Astral Receiver: The vibrational mechanism that receives and processes the influxing energies from the celestial movers into and out of the astral body. The essence within a person that receives the vibrations of the moving planets. The exact configuration of a person's Astral Receiver is indicated by the astrological chart at birth, otherwise known as the natal chart.

Astral Mechanics: The scientific study of the varying vibrational processes through which the solar system affects mankind and the earth. The manner in which to consciously adjust these energies for the benefit of all mankind. Astral mechanics is the practice of acting upon the astral schematic in order to heal and fix problematic vibrations[45].

Astral Mechanic: A person who works at the scientific practice of healing and fixing problematic vibrations that are embedded within the astral receiver.

Astral Mechanology: The study of the celestial mechanism and its effects, as they are reflected within earthborn organisms (especially but not limited to humans), the earth herself, and the weather.

---

[45] This term was coined by the brilliant genius Judith Hill. See chapter 19 for the "tenants of astro-mechanology."

Astrological Remediation: The branch of astrology that focuses on the prescription of certain herbs, foods, activities, or objects in the Earth-realm that will soothe and heal the specific needs of an individual according to their natal chart. Astrological remediation attempts to heal problematic vibrations within the energy body. It also attempts to heal karma that is interfering with the soul's well-being in this lifetime.

Some past methods of Astrological Remediation:

>Babylonia = Praying to the gods of certain planets. Performing rituals for the gods.

>Ancient Greece = Anticipating upcoming malaise in order to stoically deal with it.

>Medieval Times = Making amulets and talismans.

>Modern and Ancient India = Mantras, gems, and stones.

Conjunction: A planetary aspect in which two planets are sitting in the same place in the chart or within a few degrees of one another.

Genethliology: The study of the birth charts of individuals.

Opposition: A planetary aspect of 180 degrees.

Progression: The act of a planet in a natal chart evolving as the years go by. When a person is one year of age, the planets in that person's birth chart have progressed to the point at which they would have been sitting in the sky one day after birth. At the age of two years old, the progressions would be calculated for two days after the birth date, and so on.

Semi-sextile: A planetary aspect in which planets are 30 degrees apart.

Sextile: A planetary aspect of 60 degrees apart.

Square: A planetary aspect of 90 degrees.

Transit: The act of an orbiting planet somehow affecting and altering the qualities of a person's natal chart. More simply, a traveling planet touching a planet in the chart.

Trine: A planetary aspect of 120 degrees.

Quincunx/Inconjunct: A planetary aspect of 150 degrees.

Works Cited

Blagreve, Joseph. *The Astrological Practice of Physick.* Restored and Edited by David R. Roell. Astrology Classics, 2010

Brennan, Barbara Ann. *Hands of Light.* New York: Bantam Books, 1987

Cornell, H.L. *Encyclopaedia of Medical Astrology.* Third Edition. Maryland: Astrology Classics Publishing, 1972.

Hand, Robert. *Planets in Composite; Analyzing Human Relationships.* Schiffer Publishing, 1975

Hill, Judith. *Medical Astrology; A Guide to Planetary Pathology.* Portland, Oregon: Stellium Press, 2004

Hill, Judith. *The Astrological Body Types.* Portland, Oregon: Stellium Press, 1997

Holly, Julia, aka Judith Hill. *Mrs. Winkler's Cure.* Portland, Oregon: Stellium Press, 2010

Michelsen, Neil F. *The American Ephemeris for the 21st Century,* Starcrafts Publishing, 1997

F.A. Davis, *Taber's Cyclopedic Medical Dictionary.* Philadelphia, 2001

About Andrea L. Gehrz

Andrea Gehrz currently lives and practices astrology in Portland, Oregon. She grew up in St. Paul, Minnesota and graduated *summa cum laude* from the University of Minnesota with a Bachelor's degree in:

Individualized Studies: *focus on Cultural Studies, Identity Politics, and Family Social Sciences.*

Andrea then went on to formally study *American Sign Language Interpreting* at St. Paul Technical College. After years in the field of ASL interpreting, Andrea picked up her first Astrology book. Since that time, she has performed over 2000 readings for clients, translated two ancient Greek astrological texts, and has now written this book on the manner in which to heal problems in the astrological chart.

Andrea's first translation was an introductory book to Claudius Ptolemy's infamous and historically important text entitled the *Tetrabiblos*. Originally written by neo-platonic philosopher Porphyry of Tyre, Andrea's first book won an *Independent Publishing Book Award* in the Philosophy & Classics division in 2011. Andrea's second translation has has also received acclaim, as it is the first in a nine book Anthology written by the ancient practicing astrologer, Vettius Valens.

Andrea has also been a lifelong musician, having toured the country extensively. She started piano lessons at the age of 4, and now incorporates music into her multi-dimensional radio show entitled *The Astrological Detective*. Andrea has played in numerous bands, including *Punky Bruiser* from Minneapolis and the Portland-based two piece drum and cello duo *Discharge Information System*. She most recently has enjoyed playing drums in the technical metal/electronic duo entitled *TraumaDom*.

After birthing her daughter, Angelene, Andrea turned her astrological focus to the art of healing through the use of astrology. She has designed real-time art therapy projects matched up exactly to the charts of certain clients. Andrea attempts to heal the most challenging of struggles, as she believes the uses of astrology to be vast and profound. She currently focuses her astrological research into the areas of geniuses, children, family systems, ancient Greek translation, and Remediation. She routinely lectures for astrology groups, college associations, and spiritual centers.

She would love to hear from you!

Moira Press

www.moirapress.org

agehrz@gmail.com

971.404.5068 (Voice and VRS)

Other Books by the Moira Press

Porphyry of Tyre
An Introduction to the *Tetrabiblos*

An Introduction to the **Tetrabiblos** *of Claudius Ptolemy* was originally written in the ancient Greek language by the philosopher Porphyry of Tyre. In this ancient textbook, Porphyry sets out to clarify concepts that were left obscure in the pinnacle ancient astrological text entitled the *Tetrabiblos*. If a student of ancient Astrology were to have taken an "Astrology 101" course circa 200 A.D., this textbook could very well have been one of the books assigned during the course, along with Ptolemy's *Tetrabiblos*. This text is a must have for any beginning student of the ancient tradition of the astrological arts.

Vettius Valens of Antioch
Anthology, Book One

Vettius Valens is a historical figure in the history of Astrology. This text is an eloquent rendering of the first book in his historically profound nine-book *Anthology*. Ms. Gehrz has rendered this text into modern-day English, so that any reader can step inside the mind of an ancient practitioner of Hellenistic Astrology. This book is a pleasure to read, and any student or scholar who is interested in ancient Greece will surely be enthralled by Vettius Valens! Book one includes chapters on the planets, the constellations, the *bounds*, calculating the Midheaven by hand, the *Ascensional Times* of the signs, the manner in which to calculate *Newmoons* by hand, and much much more!

A Wonderbook of True Astrological Case Files

In this magical book of astral tales, Judith Hill and Andrea Gehrz team up to bring Astrology to the world! Each story is a simple yet eloquent example of the wonderful science of Astrology. The *Wonderbook of True Astrological Case Files* contains over 50 stories of animals with birth times, exact predictions, medical anomalies, jolly bus drivers, love contracts, tiny nooks, and much much more!

Afterwords

Astrological remediation is a vast and endless field of study. In this book, I have attempted to offer up everything I have learned from my experiences with clients, friends, and family. We here at the Moira Press look forward to future texts on healing through the use of astrology. Many people will surely contribute to the field of remediation, astro-mechanology, astrological healing, or whatever else we might decide to call the study of healing through the use of the astrological chart.

To book lectures on astrology or astrological consultations, contact the Moira Press at www.moirapress.org. We look forward to hearing from you!

-Andrea L. Gehrz
971-404-5068
Moira Press
www.moirapress.org

*of and for the advancement of
ευπορεο-αστρολογίκα*[46]

---

[46] *euporeo-astrologica*- all matters pertaining to the use of astrology to make a better life.

εὐπορέω =   1. to thrive.
2. to find a better way.
3. to have the doubts resolved.
4. to abound and have plenty.

Greek-English Lexicon Liddell and Scott p727

*Andrea L. Gehrz meets with clients
in person at her studio in Portland, Oregon.*

Book online:

MoiraPress.org

www.ingramcontent.com/pod-product-compliance
Lightning Source LLC
Chambersburg PA
CBHW070934230426
43666CB00011B/2436